Fire and Faith: Navigating the Charismatic Movement in the Modern World

Carl Davis

Published by Carl Davis, 2024.

While every precaution has been taken in the preparation of this book, the publisher assumes no responsibility for errors or omissions, or for damages resulting from the use of the information contained herein.

FIRE AND FAITH: NAVIGATING THE CHARISMATIC MOVEMENT IN THE MODERN WORLD

First edition. April 12, 2024.

ISBN: 979-8224520336

Written by Carl Davis.

Also by Carl Davis

Ek, is Dawid Soeker

A Brief History Of Christianity In Africa

Icing the Eskimo - The Art of Aggressive Sales

Nuclear Faith

Toxic Pulpit

Van Paradegrond tot Pastorie

Group Dynamics and Motivation

Pastoral counselling models for perinatal and postpartum episodes

Basic New Testament Survey

So......You want to be a Waiter

Eternal Logos: The Evolution of Scriptural Interpretation: From Ancient Methodology to Postmodern Perspectives

Ewige Woord Die Evolusie van Skrifuitleg: Van Antieke Metodiek tot Postmoderne Perspektiewe

Teaching Ministry

The Funny Side Of Reasoning - Fallacies, principles and typologies in the modern business world.

Passion Unleashed: Igniting The Future With Purpose.

Esther: Triumph of Courage and Divine Providence

Chronicles of Grace: An Epic Journey through 1 & 2 Samuel

Fire and Faith: Navigating the Charismatic Movement in the Modern World

"Fire and Faith: Navigating the Charismatic Movement in the Modern World"

Dr. Carl J. Davis
East London
South Africa
2024

"Fire and Faith: Navigating the Charismatic Movement in the Modern World"

Index:

Introduction to the Charismatic Movement

The Charismatic Movement represents a significant and vibrant expression within Christianity, emphasizing spiritual gifts, experiences of divine presence, and a fervent pursuit of the Holy Spirit's empowerment. Originating within the 20th century, this movement has profoundly impacted the landscape of global Christianity, influencing worship practices, theological perspectives, and the dynamics of Christian communities.

Origins and History

The roots of the Charismatic Movement can be traced back to the early 20th century, with the emergence of Pentecostalism, a movement marked by:

- an emphasis on the baptism of the Holy Spirit,
- speaking in tongues,
- and the operation of spiritual gifts as experienced by the early church on the day of Pentecost (Acts 2).

The Azusa Street Revival, led by William J. Seymour in Los Angeles, California, from 1906 to 1909, is often regarded as a seminal event in the Pentecostal movement, catalyzing widespread interest and enthusiasm for the manifestation of spiritual gifts and the experience of God's presence.

While Pentecostalism initially emerged as a distinct movement within Protestant Christianity, the Charismatic Movement represents a broader phenomenon transcending denominational boundaries.

In the 1960s and 1970s, there was a significant outpouring of charismatic experiences within mainline Protestant denominations, as well as within the Roman Catholic Church and other Christian traditions. This led to the proliferation of charismatic renewal movements and the integration of charismatic practices and beliefs into diverse Christian contexts.

The earliest revival movements in the charismatic church can be traced back to the 20th century, with notable events and movements that laid the foundation for the modern charismatic movement. Here are some key highlights:

Azusa Street Revival (1906-1909):

Considered one of the most significant events in the history of Pentecostalism and the charismatic movement, the Azusa Street Revival began in Los Angeles under the leadership of African-American preacher William J. Seymour. It was characterized by:

- diverse racial
- and socio-economic participation
- and a strong emphasis on spiritual gifts, especially speaking in tongues.

The revival spread Pentecostalism worldwide, laying the groundwork for the charismatic movement's later development.

Hebrides Revival (1949-1952):

The Hebrides Revival, also known as the Lewis Revival, took place in the Scottish Hebrides islands under the ministry of Duncan Campbell, a Scottish evangelist. It was marked by

- fervent prayer,
- repentance,
- and a sense of God's presence that led to widespread conversions

- and spiritual renewal, particularly among young people.

The revival had a lasting impact on the churches in Scotland and beyond, inspiring a fresh hunger for spiritual awakening.

Latter Rain Movement (1948-1950s):

The Latter Rain Movement emerged in North America, particularly in Canada and the United States, as a response to Pentecostalism's perceived institutionalization and stagnation.

It emphasized:

- the restoration of apostolic and prophetic ministries,
- the impartation of spiritual gifts,
- and the belief in a latter-day outpouring of the Holy Spirit.

Though controversial and eventually faced criticism from established Pentecostal denominations, the Latter Rain Movement contributed to developing the charismatic movement's theology and practices.

Charismatic Renewal Movement (1960s-1970s):

The Charismatic Renewal Movement began within mainline Protestant and Catholic churches in the 1960s and 1970s, as members of these denominations experienced a fresh outpouring of the Holy Spirit and charismatic gifts. Influential figures such as Dennis Bennett, an Episcopal priest, and David du Plessis, a Pentecostal leader, played critical roles in promoting the charismatic experience within these traditions.

The movement led to the widespread acceptance of charismatic practices, such as:

- speaking in tongues and healing, within traditionally non-charismatic churches,
- contributing to the growth and expansion of the charismatic movement globally.

These early revival movements in the charismatic church laid the groundwork for the broader charismatic movement that emerged in the latter half of the 20th century. They demonstrated the power of the Holy Spirit to bring about spiritual renewal, transformation, and unity across denominational boundaries, shaping the course of Christianity in the modern era.

Key Figures and Influences

Several key figures have played pivotal roles in shaping the Charismatic Movement and disseminating its teachings and practices. Among these figures, one of the most influential is Dennis Bennett, an Episcopal priest whose experience of speaking in tongues in 1960 sparked a charismatic renewal within the Episcopal Church and inspired similar movements within other mainline Protestant denominations.

Additionally, the ministry of Kathryn Kuhlman, a renowned healing evangelist known for her dynamic preaching and demonstrations of God's power, profoundly impacted the Charismatic Movement, inspiring countless individuals to seek more profound experiences of the Holy Spirit's presence and power.

In addition to these figures, the writings and teachings of Pentecostal and charismatic leaders such as:

- Oral Roberts,
- Kenneth Hagin,
- and Kenneth Copeland

have been instrumental in shaping the theological foundations and doctrinal emphases of the Charismatic Movement.

These leaders emphasized:

- the importance of faith,
- divine healing,
- and the believer's authority in Christ, influencing generations

of charismatic Christians worldwide.

The start of the charismatic church was marked by the contributions of several important figures who played significant roles in shaping its theology, practices, and growth.

Here are some of the most important figures:

William J. Seymour:

As the leader of the Azusa Street Revival in Los Angeles from 1906 to 1909, William J. Seymour is often regarded as one of the pioneers of the charismatic movement. Under his leadership, the Azusa Street Mission became a focal point for the Pentecostal revival, characterized by diverse racial and socio-economic participation, fervent worship, and manifestations of spiritual gifts such as speaking in tongues and healing.

Charles Parham:

Often referred to as the father of Pentecostalism, Charles Parham was a prominent evangelist and Bible teacher who played a vital role in the early Pentecostal movement. He founded Bethel Bible College in Topeka, Kansas, where the modern Pentecostal movement is said to have begun in 1901 with the outpouring of the Holy Spirit and speaking in tongues.

Agnes Ozman:

Agnes Ozman is credited with being the first person to speak in tongues during the modern Pentecostal movement under the ministry of Charles Parham in 1901. Her experience at Bethel Bible College in Topeka, Kansas, sparked interest and curiosity in speaking in tongues and laid the foundation for the Pentecostal and charismatic emphasis on the baptism of the Holy Spirit.

Dennis Bennett:

Dennis Bennett, an Episcopal priest, played a significant role in the Charismatic Renewal Movement of the 1960s and 1970s. In 1960, Bennett publicly testified to his experience of being baptized in the

Holy Spirit and speaking in tongues, which caused controversy within his denomination but sparked interest in charismatic experiences within mainline Protestant churches.

David du Plessis:

Known as "Mr. Pentecost" for promoting unity and cooperation among Pentecostal and charismatic Christians, David du Plessis was a South African-born Pentecostal leader who played a pivotal role in the Charismatic Renewal Movement. He worked tirelessly to bridge the gap between Pentecostal and non-Pentecostal Christians, advocating for accepting spiritual gifts and experiences across denominational lines.

Kathryn Kuhlman:

Kathryn Kuhlman was a well-known evangelist and healing minister who became one of the most influential figures in the charismatic movement during the mid-20th century. Her healing crusades, characterized by dramatic manifestations of the Holy Spirit and miraculous healings, drew large crowds and brought widespread attention to the charismatic renewal.

These figures, among others, laid the foundation for the charismatic movement, which continues to thrive and evolve today, impacting millions of believers worldwide with its emphasis on the power of the Holy Spirit, spiritual gifts, and personal encounters with God.

E.W. Kenyon

E.W. Kenyon (1867–1948) was significant in developing the Word of Faith movement.

It profoundly impacted the charismatic church through his teachings on biblical faith, the authority of the believer, and the power of confession.

Here's an overview of E.W. Kenyon and his influence on the charismatic church:

Early Life and Conversion:

Edwin (E.W.) Kenyon was born in Hadley, New York, in 1867. He grew up in a Christian home but experienced a spiritual awakening and commitment to Christ during his teenage years. Kenyon's early experiences with divine healing and the power of God's Word laid the foundation for his later ministry and teachings.

Ministry and Teachings:

E.W. Kenyon served as a pastor, evangelist, and Bible teacher, traveling extensively throughout the United States and Canada to share his message of faith and victory in Christ. He authored numerous books and pamphlets, including "The Hidden Man," "The Blood Covenant," and "Two Kinds of Righteousness," which became foundational texts for the Word of Faith movement.

Theology of Faith:

E.W. Kenyon's theology centered on "faith," which he understood as a spiritual force or creative power that could be activated through belief and confession. He taught that faith is the key to unlocking God's blessings, healing, and supernatural provision in the believer's life.

Kenyon emphasized the importance of:

- speaking God's Word in faith,
- declaring promises,
- and confessing positive affirmations to manifest desired outcomes.

Authority of the Believer:

Another critical aspect of E.W. Kenyon's teaching was the concept of the believer's authority in Christ. He emphasized that through their union with Christ, believers have been given authority over sin, sickness, and spiritual forces of darkness.

Kenyon taught that believers could exercise this authority through prayer, confession, and spiritual warfare, claiming victory in every area of life.

Influence on the Charismatic Church:

E.W. Kenyon's teachings profoundly influenced the charismatic church, particularly within the Word of Faith movement. His emphasis on faith, confession, and the believer's authority became central tenets of charismatic theology and practice.

Many charismatic leaders and ministries incorporated Kenyon's teachings into their preaching, leading to a widespread emphasis on positive confession, prosperity, and the pursuit of victory in every area of life.

Legacy and Criticism:

While E.W. Kenyon's teachings have been embraced by many within the charismatic church, they have also been subject to criticism and controversy. Critics have raised concerns about the potential for manipulation, prosperity gospel excesses, and theological errors associated with some interpretations of Kenyon's teachings. Nevertheless, his influence on the charismatic movement remains significant, shaping the beliefs and practices of millions of believers worldwide.

In summary, E.W. Kenyon was pivotal in developing the Word of Faith movement. It profoundly impacted the charismatic church through his teachings on faith, confession, and the believer's authority.

While his teachings have sparked debate and controversy, they continue to shape the theology and practice of many charismatic believers seeking to experience the fullness of God's blessings and victory in their lives.

Kenneth Hagin

Kenneth E. Hagin, often referred to as "Dad Hagin" by his followers, was a highly influential figure in the charismatic movement and a key figure in the development of the Word of Faith movement.

Here's an overview of Kenneth Hagin and his impact on the charismatic church:

Early Life and Ministry:

Kenneth Hagin was born in McKinney, Texas, on August 20, 1917. He experienced a dramatic conversion to Christianity at 15 and soon began preaching and teaching in local churches. In 1963, Hagin founded Kenneth Hagin Ministries (now known as Rhema Bible Church and Rhema Bible Training College) in Broken Arrow, Oklahoma, where he trained thousands of ministers and spread his teachings worldwide.

Word of Faith Teaching:

Kenneth Hagin is best known for his teachings on the "Word of Faith," emphasizing the power of words and the importance of speaking God's promises in faith. He believed faith is a creative force that can shape reality and achieve desired outcomes. Hagin's teachings on prosperity, healing, and the believer's authority in Christ were central to the Word of Faith movement. They influenced countless believers and ministries within the charismatic church.

Healing Ministry:

Kenneth Hagin's ministry was characterized by a strong emphasis on divine healing and miracles. He taught that healing is part of the atonement provided by Christ and that believers can appropriate God's healing power through faith and confession. Hagin's meetings often included prayer times for the sick, and many reported experiencing miraculous healings and supernatural interventions in response to his ministry.

Prophetic Ministry:

Kenneth Hagin claimed to have received numerous prophetic insights and revelations from God throughout his life. He wrote extensively on topics such as spiritual warfare, the end times, and the believer's authority, drawing from biblical scripture and his personal experiences. Hagin's prophetic ministry influenced the beliefs and practices of many within the charismatic church.

Legacy and Influence:

Kenneth Hagin's teachings have profoundly impacted the charismatic church and the broader Body of Christ. His books, tapes, and teaching materials have been translated into multiple languages and distributed worldwide, reaching millions of believers. Hagin's emphasis on faith, confession, and the power of the spoken word continues to shape the theology and practice of many charismatic ministries and churches today.

Criticism and Controversy:

While Kenneth Hagin's teachings have been embraced by many within the charismatic movement, they have also been criticized and controversial. Critics have raised concerns about the health and wealth prosperity gospel aspects of his teachings, as well as the alleged manipulation and exploitation of vulnerable believers. Some have accused Hagin of promoting a *"name it and claim it"* theology that can lead to unrealistic expectations and spiritual manipulation.

In summary, Kenneth Hagin was a central figure in the charismatic movement, known for his teachings on the Word of Faith, divine healing, and prophetic ministry. His influence continues to be felt within the charismatic church and beyond as believers worldwide continue to draw inspiration and insight from his teachings and ministry.

Oral Roberts

Oral Roberts was a pioneering figure in the charismatic movement and one of the most influential Pentecostal preachers of the 20th century.

Here's an overview of Oral Roberts and his impact on the charismatic church:

Early Life and Ministry:

Oral Roberts was born on January 24, 1918, in Pontotoc County, Oklahoma. He came from humble beginnings and experienced a conversion to Christianity at a young age. In 1947, Roberts founded the Oral Roberts Evangelistic Association, through which he launched his evangelism, healing, and media outreach ministry.

Healing Ministry:

Oral Roberts became widely known for his healing ministry, emphasizing divine healing through faith in Jesus Christ. He conducted large-scale healing crusades across the United States and worldwide, where he prayed for the sick and witnessed numerous miraculous healings. Roberts believed in the power of prayer and the laying on of hands to bring about physical, emotional, and spiritual restoration.

Television Ministry:

Oral Roberts was a pioneer in the use of television as a platform for evangelism and ministry. In 1954, he launched "Oral Roberts Presents," a weekly television program aired on local and national networks. His messages of faith, healing, and salvation reached millions of viewers. His innovative media use helped to popularize the charismatic movement and spread Pentecostal teachings to a broader audience.

Educational Legacy:

In addition to his evangelistic and healing ministry, Oral Roberts significantly impacted Christian education. In 1963, he founded Oral Roberts University (ORU) in Tulsa, Oklahoma, as a Christian liberal arts university dedicated to training students in academic excellence, spiritual growth, and service to others. ORU became a flagship institution within the charismatic movement, producing leaders and influencers in various fields of ministry, business, and the arts.

Message of Hope and Wholeness:

Oral Roberts' ministry was characterized by a message of hope, wholeness, and prosperity that resonated with believers seeking spiritual and physical healing. He taught that God desires His children to experience abundant life in every area—spiritual, physical, emotional, and financial.

Roberts' emphasis on faith, prayer, and the power of God's Word to transform lives inspired millions to pursue a deeper relationship with Christ and to expect miracles in their own lives.

Criticism and Controversy:

While Oral Roberts was highly respected within the charismatic movement, his ministry was not without controversy. Critics raised concerns about the extravagant lifestyle he and his family maintained and the perceived commercialization of his healing ministry through fundraising appeals and product sales. Additionally, some questioned the validity of his healing claims and the theological underpinnings of his prosperity gospel message.

In summary, Oral Roberts was a pioneering leader in the charismatic movement, known for his healing ministry, television outreach, educational legacy, and message of hope and wholeness.

His impact on the charismatic church and evangelical Christianity continues today, as believers worldwide draw inspiration from his teachings and ministry.

Kenneth Copeland

Kenneth Copeland is a prominent American televangelist, author, and prosperity gospel preacher who has played a significant role in the charismatic movement and evangelical Christianity.

Here's an overview of Kenneth Copeland and his impact on the charismatic church:

Early Life and Ministry Beginnings:

Kenneth Copeland was born in Lubbock, Texas, on December 6, 1936. He began his ministry in the late 1960s, initially working as a pilot for Oral Roberts and later launching his own ministry with his wife, Gloria. In 1967, he founded Kenneth Copeland Ministries (KCM) in Fort Worth, Texas, which has since become one of the world's largest and most influential television ministries.

Teaching and Emphasis on Faith and Prosperity:

Kenneth Copeland is best known for his teachings on faith, prosperity, and the power of positive confession. He espouses a form of prosperity gospel theology that teaches believers to expect financial blessings, physical healing, and success in every area of life through faith in God's promises. Copeland often emphasizes the importance of speaking God's Word and confessing His promises to activate divine favor and provision.

Media Outreach:

Kenneth Copeland Ministries has a significant media presence, with television broadcasts, radio programs, books, magazines, and online resources reaching millions worldwide. Copeland's television program, "Believer's Voice of Victory," is broadcast on various Christian networks and stations, delivering his teachings and messages to a global audience.

The ministry also hosts conferences, crusades, and events where Copeland preaches and ministers to crowds of believers.

Controversies and Criticisms:

Kenneth Copeland and his ministry have faced criticism and controversy over the years, particularly regarding their teachings on prosperity, health, and wealth. Critics argue that Copeland's emphasis on material blessings and financial prosperity can lead to a distorted understanding of the gospel and exploitation of vulnerable believers. Additionally, Copeland's lavish lifestyle, including his ownership of multiple homes, cars, and private jets, has drawn scrutiny and raised questions about the ethical implications of his teachings.

Influence and Impact:

Despite the controversies surrounding him, Kenneth Copeland has significantly influenced the charismatic church and evangelical Christianity worldwide. His teachings on faith, prosperity, and healing resonated with millions of believers seeking spiritual growth and practical guidance to live victorious lives. Copeland's ministry has also inspired many believers to pursue a deeper relationship with God and to expect supernatural manifestations of His power in their lives.

In summary, Kenneth Copeland is a prominent figure in the charismatic and evangelical churches. He is known for his faith, prosperity, and positive confession teachings. While his ministry has been marked by controversy and criticism, particularly regarding his theology and lifestyle, Copeland's influence and impact on the global Christian community cannot be denied.

John G. Lake

John G. Lake was a significant figure in the early Pentecostal and charismatic movements. He was known for his powerful healing ministry, pioneering missionary work, and emphasis on the Holy Spirit's empowerment for believers. Here's an overview of John G. Lake and his impact on the charismatic church:

Early Life and Conversion:

John Graham Lake was born on March 18, 1870, in St. Mary's, Ontario, Canada. He was raised in a Christian home but experienced a personal conversion to Christianity at the age of 16. Lake's early experiences with divine healing and spiritual encounters laid the foundation for his later ministry.

Healing Ministry:

John G. Lake's ministry was characterized by a strong emphasis on divine healing and miracles. He believed in the biblical promise of healing through faith in Jesus Christ.

He demonstrated this belief through his own healing experiences and those of others. Lake's healing campaigns drew large crowds; many testified to miraculous healings and supernatural interventions.

Missionary Work:

In addition to his healing ministry, John G. Lake was a pioneering missionary who spread Pentecostalism and the charismatic experience worldwide.

He traveled extensively throughout South Africa, establishing numerous churches, ministries, and healing rooms. Lake's missionary efforts helped to establish Pentecostalism as a global movement. They laid the groundwork for future charismatic missionaries and leaders.

The Healing Rooms:

John G. Lake is perhaps best known for establishing the "healing rooms" in Spokane, Washington, during the early 20th century. These rooms were dedicated spaces where individuals could receive prayer for healing and experience the manifest presence of God's healing power. The healing rooms became a focal point for Lake's ministry. They attracted thousands of seekers seeking physical, emotional, and spiritual restoration.

Emphasis on the Holy Spirit:

John G. Lake emphasized the vital role of the Holy Spirit in the life of the believer and the church. He believed in baptism in the Holy Spirit as a distinct experience subsequent to salvation, accompanied by the empowerment of the Spirit for ministry, spiritual gifts, and bold witness.

Lake taught that all believers could and should operate in the supernatural gifts of the Spirit, including healing, prophecy, and miracles.

Legacy and Influence:

John G. Lake's ministry and teachings have impacted the charismatic church and the broader Pentecostal movement. His emphasis on:

- divine healing,
- the Holy Spirit's empowerment,
- and the supernatural gifts of the Spirit continue to inspire believers worldwide to pursue more profound levels of faith and spiritual experience.

Many charismatic ministries and churches trace their spiritual lineage back to the influence of John G. Lake and his pioneering work in the early 20th century.

In summary, John G. Lake was a significant figure in the charismatic church, known for his powerful healing ministry, missionary endeavors, and emphasis on the Holy Spirit's empowerment for believers.

His legacy continues to inspire and challenge believers to pursue the fullness of God's presence and power in their lives and ministries.

T.L. Osborne's Healing Ministry: A Legacy of Faith and Miracles

Introduction:

T.L. Osborne was a pioneering evangelist and healer whose ministry spanned over six decades, touching countless lives worldwide with the message of salvation and healing. With a passionate commitment to spreading the gospel and demonstrating the power of God through signs and wonders, Osborne's legacy continues to inspire believers today. Let us explore T.L. Osborne's healing ministry, examining the critical elements of his approach, the impact of his work, and the enduring legacy of faith and miracles that he left behind.

Early Life and Ministry Beginnings:

Born in 1923 in India to missionary parents, T.L. Osborne grew up with a deep appreciation for the power of God and a desire to share the gospel with others. After experiencing a personal encounter with God at a young age, Osborne felt called to ministry and began preaching and evangelizing in his teens. He later married Daisy Washburn, who became his partner in ministry, and together, they embarked on a journey of faith and service that would take them to over 70 nations around the world.

Emphasis on Healing and Miracles:

Central to T.L. Osborne's ministry was his emphasis on healing and miracles as a demonstration of God's power and love. Osborne believed in the biblical promise of divine healing and saw it as an integral part of the gospel message.

He conducted healing crusades and campaigns in cities and villages across the globe, where he preached the message of salvation and prayed for the sick to be healed. Thousands experienced miraculous healings and transformations due to Osborne's ministry, testifying to the reality of God's power and presence in their lives.

Simple Faith and Bold Prayers:

One of the hallmarks of T.L. Osborne's healing ministry was his simple faith and bold prayers. Osborne believed in the power of prayer to bring about supernatural breakthroughs and was unafraid to pray for the impossible.

He encouraged believers to approach God with childlike faith, trusting His goodness and willingness to answer their prayers. Osborne's prayers were characterized by fervency, authority, and expectation, as he called upon God to intervene in miraculous ways and bring healing and wholeness to those in need.

Focus on Evangelism and Discipleship:

While healing was central to his ministry, T.L. Osborne was equally passionate about evangelism and discipleship. He saw healing as a means to an end – demonstrating God's love and power to draw people into a deeper relationship with Him.

Osborne's healing crusades were often accompanied by evangelistic efforts, where he preached the gospel message of salvation and invited people to commit their lives to Christ. He also strongly emphasized discipleship, training and equipping believers to share their faith and minister to others in their communities.

Impact and Legacy:

The impact of T.L. Osborne's healing ministry is immeasurable, with countless lives transformed by the power of God and the message of salvation.

His boldness, faith, and commitment to spreading the gospel inspire believers worldwide to step out in faith and believe in God for miracles.

Osborne's legacy lives on through the ministries of those he trained and mentored, as well as through the ongoing work of organizations like the T.L. Osborne Legacy Foundation, which seeks to continue his mission of reaching the lost and ministering to the sick and needy.

Conclusion:

T.L. Osborne's healing ministry stands as a testament to the power of God to heal, transform, and save. Through his simple faith, bold prayers, and unwavering commitment to spreading the gospel, Osborne touched the lives of millions with the message of hope and restoration.

His legacy inspires believers to pursue God's kingdom with passion and zeal, believing in miracles and trusting in His faithfulness to bring supernatural breakthroughs.

As we reflect on the life and ministry of T.L. Osborne, may we be encouraged to walk in faith, believing for God to do the impossible in our midst.

Smith Wigglesworth's Ministry: A Legacy of Faith and Miracles
Introduction:

Smith Wigglesworth was a prominent figure in the early Pentecostal and Healing Revival movements of the 20th century, known for his dynamic preaching, bold faith, and miraculous healings.

His ministry left an indelible mark on the landscape of evangelical Christianity, inspiring believers around the world to believe in the power of God to heal and transform lives.

Let us explore Smith Wigglesworth's ministry, examining the critical elements of his approach, the impact of his work, and the enduring legacy of faith and miracles that he left behind.

Early Life and Spiritual Awakening:

Born in 1859 in England, Smith Wigglesworth grew up in a family of devout Christians but did not experience a personal encounter with God until later in life.

It was not until his late twenties that Wigglesworth experienced a profound spiritual awakening, during which he was filled with the Holy Spirit and began to speak in tongues. This experience marked the beginning of Wigglesworth's ministry and set him on a path of radical faith and obedience to God.

Dynamic Preaching and Demonstrations of Power:

Central to Smith Wigglesworth's ministry was his dynamic preaching and demonstrations of God's power. Wigglesworth believed in the authority of Scripture and preached a message of repentance, salvation, and divine healing with boldness and conviction. He conducted evangelistic campaigns and healing crusades across the United Kingdom and the United States, where he proclaimed the gospel and prayed for the sick to be healed.

Wigglesworth's ministry was characterized by a remarkable display of miracles and supernatural manifestations, including the healing of the sick, the casting out of demons, and the raising of the dead. Countless testimonies attest to the miraculous interventions of God through Wigglesworth's ministry, confirming his belief in the reality of signs, wonders, and miracles as evidence of God's power and presence.

Unwavering Faith and Bold Declarations:

Smith Wigglesworth was known for his unwavering faith and bold declarations of God's promises. He believed in the believer's authority to exercise faith and command healing and deliverance in Jesus' name. Wigglesworth often exhorted believers to stand on the promises of Scripture, to expect God to intervene supernaturally in their lives, and to declare victory over sickness, sin, and spiritual bondage.

Wigglesworth's faith was tested and proven repeatedly through his encounters with adversity and opposition. Despite facing opposition from skeptics, critics, and even members of the medical profession,

Wigglesworth remained steadfast in his conviction that God was able to do exceedingly abundantly above all that we ask or think.

Legacy and Influence:

The impact of Smith Wigglesworth's ministry continues to resonate within the global Christian community, inspiring believers to pursue God's kingdom with faith, boldness, and expectancy.

His life and ministry have been commemorated through books, biographies, and documentaries that document his remarkable feats of faith and the enduring legacy of miracles that he left behind.

Wigglesworth's teachings on faith, healing, and the Holy Spirit influence generations of believers, challenging them to step out in faith and believe in God for the impossible. His example of radical obedience and unwavering trust in God's promises is a powerful reminder of the transformative power of faith when coupled with the power of the Holy Spirit.

Conclusion:

Smith Wigglesworth's ministry stands as a testament to the power of God to work miracles and transform lives through the hands of yielded vessels.

His boldness, faith, and unwavering trust in God's promises inspire believers to believe in the supernatural and step out in faith, expecting God to move in miraculous ways. As we reflect on the life and ministry of Smith Wigglesworth, may we be challenged to pursue God's kingdom with the same fervor, faith, and expectancy, trusting in His power to do exceedingly abundantly above all that we ask or think.

Benny Hinn

Benny Hinn is a prominent televangelist, preacher, and author who has played a significant role in the charismatic church over the past several decades.

Known for his dynamic preaching style, emphasis on divine healing, and large-scale evangelistic events, Hinn has profoundly impacted the charismatic movement worldwide.

Here's an overview of the role Benny Hinn has played in the charismatic church:

Early Life and Ministry Beginnings:

Benny Hinn was born on December 3, 1952, in Jaffa, Israel, to a family of Greek and Armenian descent. He grew up in a Christian household and developed a passion for evangelism and ministry from a young age. Hinn's ministry began in the 1970s when he started traveling and preaching at churches and evangelistic events across the United States and worldwide.

Teaching and Emphasis on Healing:

One of Benny Hinn's hallmark teachings is his emphasis on divine healing and the supernatural power of God to bring about physical, emotional, and spiritual wholeness.

Hinn often incorporates stories of miraculous healings and testimonies into his preaching, encouraging believers to expect and receive healing through faith in Jesus Christ.

His ministry has been characterized by large-scale healing crusades and revival meetings where attendees report experiencing supernatural manifestations and healings.

Media and Technology:

Benny Hinn is known for his extensive use of media and technology to reach a global audience with his message. He hosts the "This Is Your Day" television program on various Christian networks worldwide, reaching millions of viewers with his teachings, testimonies, and messages of hope and encouragement.

Hinn also utilizes social media platforms, websites, and mobile apps to engage with his followers and disseminate his ministry content.

Controversies and Criticisms:

Throughout his career, Benny Hinn has been the subject of controversy and criticism, both within and outside the charismatic church. Critics have raised concerns about his theology, financial practices, and extravagant lifestyle, including owning multiple luxury homes, cars, and private jets.

Hinn has faced accusations of promoting a prosperity gospel message that focuses on material blessings and financial prosperity rather than the true gospel of salvation through Jesus Christ.

Impact and Influence:

Despite the controversies surrounding him, Benny Hinn has significantly impacted the charismatic church and evangelical Christianity worldwide.

His ministry has reached millions through television, radio, the internet, and live events, leading many to faith in Christ and encouraging believers to pursue a deeper relationship with God. Hinn's emphasis on divine healing and the supernatural has also contributed to the growth and expansion of the charismatic movement, inspiring believers to expect and experience the power of God in their lives.

In summary, Benny Hinn has played a prominent role in the charismatic church through his dynamic preaching, emphasis on divine healing, extensive media outreach, and global influence. While his ministry has been marked by controversy and criticism, Hinn's impact on the charismatic movement and evangelical Christianity cannot be denied, as he continues to reach millions of people with his message of faith, healing, and hope.

Rodney Howard-Browne

Rodney Howard-Browne is a South African-born charismatic Christian preacher known for his role in the charismatic movement, particularly for his ministry of revival meetings.

He gained international prominence in the 1990s for his involvement in what became known as the "Toronto Blessing" and the "Laughing Revival."

Here's an overview of Rodney Howard-Browne and his impact on the charismatic church, mainly through revival meetings:

Early Life and Ministry:

Rodney Howard-Browne was born in Port Elizabeth, South Africa, in 1961. He grew up in a Pentecostal family and felt a calling to ministry from a young age. Howard-Browne's ministry journey took him from South Africa to the United States, where he eventually founded Revival Ministries International (RMI) and the River at Tampa Bay Church in Tampa, Florida.

Anointing for Revival:

Rodney Howard-Browne became known for his emphasis on revival and spiritual awakening, which he believed could be experienced through the "anointing" or "impartation" of the Holy Spirit.

He often preached on the necessity of being filled with the Spirit and experiencing the tangible presence of God, which he claimed could lead to personal transformation and revival on a larger scale.

Toronto Blessing and Laughing Revival:

In the early 1990s, Rodney Howard-Browne's ministry gained widespread attention due to his involvement in what came to be known as the "Toronto Blessing" and the "Laughing Revival."

These revival meetings were characterized by manifestations of spiritual phenomena such as laughter, shaking, crying, and falling under the power of the Spirit. While controversial, these meetings attracted thousands of believers seeking a fresh encounter with God. They sparked debates within the charismatic community about the nature of revival and spiritual manifestations.

Revival Meetings and Crusades:

Rodney Howard-Browne's ministry is marked by a focus on hosting revival meetings, crusades, and conferences worldwide.

These events typically feature dynamic worship, passionate preaching, and opportunities for prayer and ministry. Howard-Browne often emphasizes the importance of faith, expectancy, and hunger for God's presence as prerequisites for experiencing a revival and spiritual breakthrough.

Criticism and Controversy:

While Rodney Howard-Browne's ministry has drawn thousands of followers and supporters, it has also faced criticism and controversy within the broader Christian community. Critics have raised concerns about the authenticity of the spiritual manifestations observed in revival meetings and the theological implications of some of Howard-Browne's teachings and practices.

Additionally, some have questioned the long-term fruitfulness and impact of revival meetings focusing primarily on emotional experiences rather than discipleship and biblical teaching.

Global Impact:

Despite the controversy surrounding his ministry, Rodney Howard-Browne has significantly impacted the charismatic church worldwide.

His revival meetings and conferences have attracted believers from diverse backgrounds and denominations, fostering a sense of unity and expectancy for revival within the body of Christ.

Howard-Browne's emphasis on the power and presence of the Holy Spirit has inspired many believers to seek a deeper relationship with God and pursue personal revival in their lives.

Rodney Howard-Browne has played a significant role in the charismatic church, mainly through his ministry, which focused on revival meetings and spiritual awakening.

While his methods and teachings have sparked controversy and debate, his emphasis on the Holy Spirit's power and presence has encouraged believers to hunger for God's move in their lives and the world.

Creflo Dollar

Creflo Dollar is a prominent American pastor, televangelist, and founder of the World Changers Church International, a charismatic megachurch in College Park, Georgia.

He is known for his dynamic preaching style, emphasis on prosperity gospel teachings, and global ministry outreach.

Here's an overview of Creflo Dollar and his influence within the charismatic church:

Early Life and Ministry:

Creflo Dollar was born in College Park, Georgia, on January 28, 1962. He received a Bachelor of Science in education from West Georgia College and a Bachelor of Arts in biblical studies from the International Bible Institute and Seminary.

In 1986 he founded World Changers Ministries Christian Center, which later became World Changers Church International.

World Changers Church International:

Founded in 1986, World Changers Church International has grown into a global ministry with satellite churches and missions worldwide.

The church's headquarters, located in College Park, Georgia, boasts a large campus with a capacity of thousands of worshippers.

Creflo Dollar serves as the church's senior pastor, attracting a diverse congregation with its contemporary worship style and practical teaching.

Prosperity Gospel Teaching:

Creflo Dollar is known for his teachings on the prosperity gospel, emphasizing that financial prosperity and physical well-being are part of God's plan for believers.

He teaches that through faith, confession, and sowing financial seeds, believers can expect blessings and abundance from God. Dollar's teachings often center on faith, confession, and the power of positive thinking to manifest desired outcomes.

Media Ministry:

Creflo Dollar's ministry extends beyond the walls of his church through various media platforms.

He hosts the "Changing Your World" program on networks such as TBN and Daystar. Dollar's sermons and teachings are also widely distributed through books, DVDs, podcasts, and online streaming platforms, reaching millions of viewers and listeners worldwide.

Controversies and Criticisms:

While Creflo Dollar's ministry has garnered a large following and impacted many lives, it has also faced criticism and controversy.

Some critics have raised concerns about his teachings on the prosperity gospel, questioning the emphasis on material wealth and the theology of giving to receive.

Dollar has also faced scrutiny over his personal finances and lifestyle, including his ownership of private jets and lavish properties.

Philanthropic Work:

Despite the controversies surrounding his ministry, Creflo Dollar is involved in various philanthropic initiatives through his ministry.

World Changers Church International supports outreach programs, mission work, and charitable endeavors domestically and internationally. Dollar has been involved in disaster relief efforts, community development projects, and initiatives to combat poverty and social injustice.

In summary, Creflo Dollar is a prominent figure within the charismatic church. It is known for its dynamic preaching, emphasis on prosperity gospel teachings, and global ministry outreach.

While his ministry has faced criticism and controversy, particularly regarding his teachings on prosperity, Dollar continues to impact millions of lives through his media ministry, philanthropic work, and commitment to spreading the message of faith and empowerment.

Dr. Bill Winston

Dr. Bill Winston is a highly influential figure within the charismatic Christian community. He is known for his dynamic preaching, emphasis on faith, and commitment to empowering believers to live victorious lives.

Here's an overview of Bill Winston and his impact within the charismatic church:

Background and Education:

Bill Winston was born in Tuskegee, Alabama, and raised in the church. He holds a Bachelor of Science degree in Industrial Engineering from Tuskegee Institute (now Tuskegee University) and a Master's degree in Business Administration from the University of Detroit. He also earned a Doctor of Ministry degree from Friends International Christian University.

Ministry Leadership:

In 1986, Bill Winston founded Living Word Christian Center in Forest Park, Illinois, where he serves as the senior pastor.

Under his leadership, Living Word Christian Center has grown into a thriving multicultural congregation with thousands of members.

The church is known for its vibrant worship services, emphasis on faith-based teaching, and commitment to community outreach and discipleship.

Faith-Based Teaching:

Bill Winston is renowned for his powerful teaching on the subject of faith. He emphasizes the importance of understanding and applying biblical principles of faith to every area of life, including finances, health, relationships, and career.

His teaching is rooted in Scripture, particularly passages such as Mark 11:22-24, which speaks of the power of faith to move mountains and bring about supernatural results.

Kingdom Principles:

In addition to faith, Bill Winston teaches the principles of the Kingdom of God and the believer's authority as sons and daughters of God.

He emphasizes the importance of believers understanding their identity in Christ and walking in the authority and power that comes from being seated with Christ in heavenly places (Ephesians 2:6).

Media Ministry:

Bill Winston's ministry extends beyond the walls of his church through various media platforms. He hosts the television program "Believer's Walk of Faith," which airs on national and international networks, reaching millions of viewers around the world.

His sermons and teachings are also widely distributed through books, DVDs, podcasts, and online streaming platforms.

Impact and Influence:

Bill Winston's ministry has had a significant impact within the charismatic church and beyond. His teachings on faith, the Kingdom of God, and spiritual authority have inspired countless believers to live with confidence, boldness, and expectation of God's supernatural intervention in their lives.

He is respected as a spiritual father and mentor to many pastors and leaders within the charismatic community.

Community Engagement:

In addition to his ministry work, Bill Winston is actively involved in community outreach and development initiatives.

Through the Joseph Business School, founded by Bill Winston, individuals are equipped with practical skills and biblical principles for success in business and entrepreneurship.

He also supports various humanitarian efforts and initiatives to address social issues and empower disadvantaged communities.

In summary, Bill Winston is a highly respected leader and teacher within the Charismatic church, known for his emphasis on faith, Kingdom principles, and empowering believers to live victorious lives.

His ministry has impacted millions worldwide, inspiring believers to walk in their God-given authority and experience the abundant life Jesus promised.

Joyce Meyer

Joyce Meyer is a prominent figure in the Christian community, particularly within the charismatic and evangelical traditions.

Known for her practical teaching, candid storytelling, and emphasis on personal growth and empowerment, Joyce Meyer has become one of the most recognized and influential Christian speakers and authors worldwide.

Here's an overview of her life and ministry:

Early Life and Background:

Joyce Meyer was born on June 4, 1943, in St. Louis, Missouri. She had a difficult childhood marked by sexual abuse, dysfunction, and personal struggles. After experiencing a profound spiritual awakening at 9, Joyce Meyer committed to serving God and embarked on personal transformation and healing.

Ministry Beginnings:

In 1976, Joyce Meyer began teaching the Bible in small group settings. She eventually started her own ministry, initially called "Life in the Word."

Over the years, her ministry expanded through radio broadcasts, television programs, and speaking engagements, reaching millions worldwide with her message of hope, faith, and practical wisdom.

Teaching Ministry:

Joyce Meyer's teaching ministry focuses on applying biblical principles to everyday life. She addresses overcoming adversity, managing emotions, developing healthy relationships, and experiencing personal growth and transformation.

Her teaching style is characterized by authenticity, transparency, and humor as she shares personal anecdotes and insights from her life journey.

Emphasis on Renewing the Mind:

One of Joyce Meyer's core teachings is renewing the mind according to biblical truth. She emphasizes the power of positive thinking, confession, and meditation on Scripture to overcome negative thought patterns and experience lasting change.

Her book "Battlefield of the Mind" has become a bestseller and a staple resource for many seeking to overcome mental and emotional struggles.

Outreach and Humanitarian Work:

In addition to her teaching ministry, Joyce Meyer is actively involved in humanitarian efforts and outreach programs worldwide.

Through Joyce Meyer Ministries, she supports initiatives such as feeding programs, disaster relief efforts, and education and vocational training for disadvantaged communities. Her ministry is committed to positively impacting the lives of those in need spiritually and practically.

Criticism and Controversy:

Joyce Meyer has faced criticism and controversy over the years despite her widespread popularity and influence. Some have raised concerns about her teachings on prosperity and financial prosperity gospel, questioning the emphasis on material wealth and the theology of giving to receive. Others have criticized her lavish lifestyle, including owning multiple homes and expensive possessions.

Legacy and Impact:

Regardless of the criticism, Joyce Meyer's ministry has left a significant legacy impacting countless lives worldwide.

Through her books, television programs, conferences, and outreach efforts, she has inspired millions to grow in their faith, overcome obstacles, and live with purpose and passion.

Her transparent approach to sharing her struggles and victories has resonated with people from all walks of life, making her a beloved and respected figure in the Christian community.

In summary, Joyce Meyer is a highly influential Christian speaker, author, and teacher known for her practical wisdom, transparent storytelling, and commitment to empowering individuals to live their best lives through faith in God. Her ministry continues to reach millions worldwide, offering hope, encouragement, and transformational teaching grounded in the truth of God's Word.

Joel Osteen

Joel Osteen is a prominent American pastor, author, and televangelist known for his positive and uplifting messages that have inspired millions worldwide.

Here's an overview of Joel Osteen and his impact on the Christian community:

Early Life and Ministry:

Joel Osteen was born to John and Dodie Osteen in Houston, Texas, on March 5, 1963. His father, John Osteen, was the founder and senior pastor of Lakewood Church, a charismatic megachurch in Houston.

After his father died in 1999, Joel assumed the senior pastor role at Lakewood Church despite having no formal theological training.

Leadership at Lakewood Church:

Under Joel Osteen's leadership, Lakewood Church experienced significant growth, becoming one of the largest and most influential churches in the United States.

The church moved to the former Compaq Center, a sports arena in Houston, to accommodate its growing congregation. Lakewood Church's weekly services attract tens of thousands of attendees and millions of viewers through television and online broadcasts.

Positive Message and Teaching:

Joel Osteen is known for his positive and uplifting messages that focus on hope, faith, and the power of positive thinking. He often emphasizes the importance of maintaining a positive attitude, trusting God's plan, and speaking words of faith and victory over one's life. Osteen's teaching style is conversational and relatable, making complex spiritual concepts accessible to a broad audience.

Bestselling Author:

In addition to his preaching ministry, Joel Osteen is a bestselling author who has written numerous books on faith, personal growth, and living a fulfilled life.

His books, including "Your Best Life Now" and "The Power of I Am," have sold millions of copies worldwide and have been translated into multiple languages. Osteen's books offer practical advice and spiritual insights to help readers overcome challenges and live their best lives.

Media Ministry:

Joel Osteen's ministry extends beyond the walls of Lakewood Church through various media platforms. He hosts the weekly television program "Joel Osteen Ministries," which airs in over 100 countries and reaches millions of viewers each week.

In addition to television, Osteen's sermons and teachings are available through podcasts, online streaming platforms, and social media channels, making his messages accessible to a global audience.

Criticism and Controversy:

Despite his widespread popularity and influence, Joel Osteen has faced criticism and controversy. Some critics have accused him of preaching a "prosperity gospel," emphasizing material wealth and success as signs of God's favor.

Others have questioned his theology and teaching style, arguing that it lacks depth and fails to address the complexities of life and faith.

Philanthropic Work:

In addition to his ministry efforts, Joel Osteen is actively involved in philanthropic work and community outreach initiatives. Lakewood Church supports various humanitarian projects, including feeding programs, disaster relief efforts, and initiatives to combat homelessness and poverty.

Osteen and his wife, Victoria, are committed to positively impacting their community and helping those in need.

In summary, Joel Osteen is a highly influential pastor, author, and speaker known for his positive message of hope, faith, and personal empowerment. Through his leadership at Lakewood Church, bestselling books, and media ministry, Osteen has inspired millions to live with faith, courage, and optimism in life's challenges. While he has faced criticism and controversy, his impact within the Christian community and beyond is undeniable as he continues to spread messages of encouragement and inspiration to people worldwide.

T. D. Jakes:

Bishop T. D. Jakes is The Potter's House's founder and senior pastor, a megachurch in Dallas, Texas, with a global outreach ministry.

Known for his powerful preaching and motivational speaking, Jakes addresses various topics, including faith, leadership, and personal development. He is also a bestselling author and filmmaker who significantly influences the charismatic community and mainstream culture.

Bill Johnson:

Bill Johnson is the senior leader of Bethel Church in Redding, California, and the leader of Bethel Music, a Christian music label associated with the church.

Known for his emphasis on supernatural ministry, prophetic worship, and the kingdom of God, Johnson's teachings have profoundly impacted the charismatic movement worldwide. Bethel Church is also known for its School of Supernatural Ministry, which trains students in supernatural ministry and revival culture.

Brian Houston:

Brian Houston is the founder and senior pastor of Hillsong Church, a global network of charismatic churches in cities worldwide. Under Houston's leadership, Hillsong has become known for its contemporary worship music, vibrant youth ministry, and emphasis on creative expression.

Houston's influence extends beyond the church as a bestselling author and speaker, addressing leadership, faith, and personal growth.

Joseph Prince:

Joseph Prince is the senior pastor of New Creation Church in Singapore, one of the largest megachurches in Asia.

He is known for his grace-centered teaching, which emphasizes the unmerited favor of God and the finished work of Jesus Christ. Prince's televised sermons and bestselling books have reached a global audience, making him one of the most influential charismatic preachers in the world today.

Steven Furtick:

Steven Furtick is the founding pastor of Elevation Church, a multisite megachurch based in Charlotte, North Carolina.

Known for his dynamic preaching style and creative approach to ministry, Furtick has built Elevation Church into one of the fastest-growing churches in the United States.

He is also a bestselling author and speaker, addressing faith, leadership, and personal development topics.

Todd White

Todd White is a prominent Christian evangelist, author, and founder of Lifestyle Christianity. This ministry empowers believers to live out their faith daily.

Known for his bold approach to evangelism and emphasis on supernatural encounters, Todd White has inspired countless individuals to step out in faith and share the love of Jesus Christ with others.

Here's an overview of Todd White and his impact on the Christian community:

Early Life and Conversion:

Todd White was born in Longview, Texas, on May 21, 1975. He grew up in a non-religious family and lived a life marked by drug addiction and rebellion.

In 2004, Todd's life-changing encounter with God led to his conversion to Christianity.

He renounced his former lifestyle and devoted himself to following Jesus Christ wholeheartedly.

Ministry Beginnings:

After his conversion, Todd White felt called to share the gospel with others and began evangelizing on the streets, parks, and public places.

He gained attention for his boldness and compassion in reaching out to people with the message of God's love and healing power. Todd's ministry quickly grew as testimonies of miraculous healings and supernatural encounters began to spread.

Lifestyle Christianity:

In 2011, Todd White founded Lifestyle Christianity, a ministry dedicated to training and equipping believers to live out their faith authentically in their daily lives.

The ministry focuses on evangelism, discipleship, and demonstrating the power of God's love through supernatural signs and wonders. Lifestyle Christianity offers training programs, conferences, and resources to empower believers to step into their identity as sons and daughters of God and share the gospel with boldness and compassion.

Emphasis on Healing and Miracles:

Todd White's ministry is characterized by a strong emphasis on healing and miracles. He believes in the power of God to supernaturally heal the sick, restore broken lives, and set people free from bondage.

Todd often prays for healing for individuals during his evangelistic outreaches and sees many remarkable testimonies of God's miraculous intervention.

Controversy and Criticism:

Despite his widespread popularity and impact, Todd White's ministry has faced criticism and controversy from some within the Christian community.

Critics have raised concerns about his theology, particularly regarding the emphasis on signs and wonders and the manifestation of supernatural gifts. Some have questioned the authenticity of the healings and miracles reported in Todd's ministry. In contrast, others have reservations about his methods and approach to evangelism.

Commitment to Love and Compassion:

Despite the criticism, Todd White remains committed to spreading God's love and compassion to all people. He emphasizes the importance of loving others unconditionally, regardless of their background, beliefs, or lifestyle choices.

Todd believes that the most excellent demonstration of God's power is found in love, and he seeks to reflect that love in his interactions with everyone he encounters.

Global Impact:

Todd White's ministry has had a global impact, reaching people from all walks of life and cultural backgrounds.

He travels extensively, speaking at churches, conferences, and events worldwide, and his teachings and testimonies are widely shared through social media and online platforms.

Todd's passion for evangelism and discipleship has inspired many to step out in faith and make a difference in their communities and nations.

In summary, Todd White is a dynamic evangelist and founder of Lifestyle Christianity. He is known for his bold approach to sharing the gospel and emphasizing supernatural encounters.

Despite facing criticism and controversy, Todd remains committed to spreading God's love and healing power to the ends of the earth, empowering believers to live out their faith with passion and authenticity.

His ministry continues to impact lives worldwide, drawing people into a deeper relationship with Jesus Christ and transforming communities through the power of the gospel.

Todd Bentley

Todd Bentley is a controversial figure in the charismatic Christian community. He is known for his involvement in the charismatic revival movement and his unique approach to ministry, including claims of miraculous healings and supernatural encounters.

Here's an overview of Todd Bentley and his impact within the charismatic church:

Early Life and Conversion:

Todd Bentley was born on January 10, 1976, in Canada. He grew up in a troubled environment, experiencing abuse, addiction, and homelessness during his teenage years.

In his early twenties, Bentley had a profound encounter with God, leading to his conversion to Christianity and a dramatic transformation of his life.

Ministry Beginnings:

Todd Bentley rose to prominence in the early 2000s as a charismatic evangelist and revivalist. He gained attention for his unconventional style of ministry, which included passionate preaching, fervent prayer, and dramatic manifestations of the Holy Spirit. Bentley became known for his involvement in the Lakeland Revival in 2008, a series of charismatic meetings in Florida that drew thousands of attendees and garnered widespread media coverage.

Healing Ministry:

One of Todd Bentley's primary ministry focuses has been healing and miracles.

He claims to have witnessed numerous miraculous healings and supernatural manifestations in his meetings, including blind eyes being opened, deaf ears being unstopped, and people being miraculously delivered from physical ailments and demonic oppression.

Bentley often emphasizes the power of faith and prayer to bring about these supernatural encounters.

Controversy and Criticism:

Despite his popularity within specific segments of the charismatic community, Todd Bentley's ministry has been marked by controversy and criticism.

He has faced allegations of financial misconduct, sexual impropriety, and theological errors. In 2008, Bentley's ministry came under scrutiny after reports surfaced of his involvement in an extramarital affair and subsequent divorce. The controversy led to the suspension of the Lakeland Revival and raised questions about Bentley's credibility as a minister.

Restoration and Continued Ministry:

In the years following the Lakeland Revival, Todd Bentley has continued to minister, albeit with a lower profile and under closer scrutiny.

He has publicly acknowledged his past mistakes and expressed remorse for the pain and hurt caused to others.

Bentley has undergone a process of restoration and reconciliation with certain church leaders and ministries who have supported his continued ministry efforts.

Current Activities:

In recent years, Todd Bentley has been involved in various ministry endeavors, including hosting conferences, leading revival meetings, and participating in media outreach.

He emphasizes healing, deliverance, and supernatural encounters in his ministry, often drawing on his own personal experiences and testimonies of others to illustrate God's power at work.

Critical Evaluation:

While some within the charismatic community support Todd Bentley and his ministry, others have raised concerns about his teachings, practices, and character.

Critics caution against uncritical acceptance of miraculous claims and urge discernment in evaluating Bentley's ministry in light of biblical truth and accountability within the body of Christ.

In summary, Todd Bentley is a polarizing figure within the charismatic Christian community. He is known for his charismatic personality, passionate preaching, and claims of supernatural encounters. While his ministry has garnered supporters and detractors, Bentley's impact within the charismatic church continues to provoke debate and reflection on the nature of revival, healing, and the operation of spiritual gifts in the modern church.

Definition of Charismatic Christianity

Charismatic Christianity can be broadly defined as a theological perspective and spiritual orientation within Christianity that emphasizes the ongoing work of the Holy Spirit in the lives of believers, the manifestation of spiritual gifts, and the experiential dimension of faith.

At its core, charismatic Christianity affirms the belief that the same Holy Spirit who empowered the early church in the book of Acts continues to work in and through believers today, empowering them for ministry and service.

One of the defining features of charismatic Christianity is the emphasis on spiritual gifts, which are understood as special abilities or manifestations of the Holy Spirit given to believers to build up the body of Christ and advance God's kingdom on earth.

As outlined in the New Testament, these gifts include prophecy, healing, tongues, interpretation of tongues, miracles, discernment, and others (1 Corinthians 12:4-11).

Another central aspect of charismatic Christianity is the emphasis on experiential encounters with God's presence and power, often manifested through prayer, worship, laying on of hands, and the ministry of the Holy Spirit.

Charismatic Christians highly value personal experiences of God's love, grace, and power, viewing them as essential components of authentic faith and spiritual growth.

Furthermore, charismatic Christianity is characterized by a strong sense of expectation and anticipation for the supernatural intervention of God in the lives of believers and the world at large. Charismatic Christians believe in the reality of divine healing, deliverance from spiritual bondage, and the fulfillment of prophetic promises, viewing these as tangible expressions of God's kingdom breaking into the present age.

In summary, the Charismatic Movement represents a dynamic and diverse expression of Christianity, emphasizing spiritual gifts, experiential encounters with God, and a fervent pursuit of the Holy Spirit's empowerment.

With its roots in the early 20th-century Pentecostal movement and its ongoing influence within Protestant, Catholic, and other Christian traditions, the Charismatic Movement continues to shape the beliefs, practices, and spiritual experiences of millions worldwide.

Theological Foundations of the Charismatic Movement

The Charismatic Movement is deeply rooted in theological foundations that shape its beliefs, practices, and worldview. At the heart of charismatic theology are core doctrines related to the person and work of the Holy Spirit, the manifestation of spiritual gifts, and the importance of these gifts in the life of the believer and the church.

In this comprehensive exploration, we will delve into the theological underpinnings of the Charismatic Movement, focusing on the doctrine of the Holy Spirit, the gifts of the Spirit, and their significance in charismatic theology.

Doctrine of the Holy Spirit

Central to charismatic theology is the doctrine of the Holy Spirit, which emphasizes the third person of the Trinity as the active agent in the life of the believer and the church. Charismatic Christians affirm the biblical teaching that the Holy Spirit is entirely God, co-equal with the Father and the Son, and possesses divine attributes and authority.

The doctrine of the Holy Spirit encompasses several critical theological concepts:

Personhood of the Holy Spirit:

Charismatic theology affirms the personhood of the Holy Spirit, recognizing Him as a distinct and personal being with intellect, emotions, and will. The Holy Spirit is not an impersonal force or influence but a divine person who can be known, experienced, and interacted with in a personal relationship.

Deity of the Holy Spirit:

Charismatic theology upholds the deity of the Holy Spirit, affirming His divine nature and attributes. The Holy Spirit shares in the divine essence and possesses the same divine attributes as the Father and the Son, including omniscience, omnipotence, and omnipresence.

Work of the Holy Spirit:

Charismatic theology emphasizes the multifaceted work of the Holy Spirit in the world and in the lives of believers. This work includes regeneration (John 3:5-8), sanctification (2 Thessalonians 2:13), empowerment for ministry (Acts 1:8), and the indwelling presence of God in the believer (Romans 8:9-11).

Filling of the Holy Spirit:

Charismatic theology teaches believers to experience a distinct and ongoing filling or empowerment of the Holy Spirit for effective ministry and spiritual growth. This filling is not a one-time event but a continuous process of surrendering to the Spirit's leading and allowing Him to work in and through the believer's life.

Baptism of the Holy Spirit:

Charismatic theology specializes in the baptism of the Holy Spirit as a distinct experience after conversion, often accompanied by the manifestation of spiritual gifts, such as speaking in tongues (Acts 2:4) and prophecy (Acts 2:17-18). This baptism is viewed as a separate and empowering encounter with the Spirit for service and witness.

Gifts of the Spirit

Another cornerstone of charismatic theology is believing in the ongoing manifestation of spiritual gifts within the church. Charismatic Christians affirm the biblical teaching that the Holy Spirit distributes various gifts to believers to edify the body of Christ and advance God's kingdom on earth.

The gifts of the Spirit, as outlined in the New Testament, include:

Word of Wisdom:

The ability to receive and communicate divine wisdom and insight for specific situations or circumstances (1 Corinthians 12:8).

Word of Knowledge:

The ability to receive supernatural knowledge or understanding about a person, situation, or event through the Holy Spirit (1 Corinthians 12:8).

Faith:

A supernatural gift of faith that enables believers to trust God for miraculous outcomes or to believe in the impossible (1 Corinthians 12:9).

Healing:

The ability to pray for and witness miraculous healings and supernatural physical, emotional, or spiritual interventions (1 Corinthians 12:9).

Miracles:

The ability to perform supernatural acts or signs that defy natural laws and demonstrate God's power and authority (1 Corinthians 12:10).

Prophecy:

The ability to speak forth a message from God for edification, exhortation, or comfort (1 Corinthians 14:3).

Discerning of Spirits:

The ability to discern the presence and activity of spiritual forces, including angels, demons, and the Holy Spirit, in a given situation (1 Corinthians 12:10).

Speaking in Tongues:

The ability to speak in a language unknown to the speaker often accompanied by interpretation for the edification of the church (1 Corinthians 12:10).

Interpretation of Tongues:

The ability to interpret messages spoken in tongues for the benefit of the church community (1 Corinthians 12:10).

Importance of Spiritual Gifts in Charismatic Theology

In charismatic theology, spiritual gifts are viewed as essential tools for building up the body of Christ, equipping believers for ministry, and demonstrating the power and presence of God in the world.

These gifts are not limited to a select few individuals. Still, they are distributed by the Holy Spirit to all believers according to His sovereign will and purpose.

Charismatic theology emphasizes the importance of cultivating and exercising spiritual gifts within the context of the local church community.

Believers are encouraged to earnestly desire spiritual gifts (1 Corinthians 14:1), to seek the edification of the church above personal gratification (1 Corinthians 14:12), and to exercise spiritual gifts in love and humility (1 Corinthians 13).

Furthermore, charismatic theology recognizes the dynamic and multifaceted nature of spiritual gifts. It acknowledges that the Holy Spirit may distribute different gifts to believers according to their unique calling, personality, and ministry context. While some gifts may be more visible or spectacular than others, all gifts are valued and necessary for the healthy functioning of the body of Christ.

In summary, the doctrine of the Holy Spirit and the manifestation of spiritual gifts are foundational elements of charismatic theology, shaping its beliefs, practices, and understanding of the Christian life.

Charismatic Christians affirm the personhood and deity of the Holy Spirit, recognize the ongoing work of the Spirit in the world, and eagerly pursue the manifestation of spiritual gifts to build up the body of Christ and advance God's kingdom on earth.

The broader Charismatic Doctrine

The formation of charismatic doctrine has been influenced by various secular factors throughout history, including cultural trends, social movements, and philosophical ideas.

While charismatic theology is primarily rooted in biblical interpretation and spiritual experiences, it has also been shaped by the broader cultural context in which it emerged. Here are some of the secular influences on the formation of charismatic doctrine:

Cultural Context:

Charismatic doctrine has been influenced by the cultural context in which it developed. For example, the charismatic movement emerged in the mid-20th century during social upheaval and cultural change, including the civil rights movement, the sexual revolution, and the countercultural movements of the 1960s.

These cultural shifts influenced the ethos of the charismatic movement, shaping its emphasis on personal experience, authenticity, and freedom of expression.

Psychological and Emotional Factors:

Psychological and emotional factors can influence the emphasis on spiritual experiences and manifestations in charismatic doctrine.

For example, the desire for emotional fulfillment, psychological healing, and personal empowerment can drive individuals to seek out charismatic experiences to find meaning, purpose, and emotional support in their lives.

Media and Technology:

The spread of charismatic doctrine has been facilitated by advancements in media and technology, including television, radio, the internet, and social media.

Charismatic preachers and ministries utilize these platforms to broadcast their messages, reach broader audiences, and engage with believers worldwide. The influence of media and technology on charismatic doctrine can be seen in charismatic leaders' and ministries' presentation styles, communication strategies, and branding techniques.

Consumer Culture:

Charismatic doctrine has been influenced by consumer culture, with its emphasis on individual choice, personal fulfillment, and instant gratification.

Charismatic churches and ministries often adopt marketing techniques, branding strategies, and consumer-oriented approaches to attract and retain members. The focus on material blessings, financial prosperity, and success in charismatic teaching can also reflect consumerist values and aspirations.

Globalization and Diversity:

The globalization of the charismatic movement has led to the exchange of ideas, practices, and theological perspectives across cultural, geographical, and linguistic boundaries. Charismatic doctrine has been enriched by the diversity of global Christianity, incorporating elements from different cultural traditions, theological perspectives, and spiritual practices.

At the same time, globalization has also led to tensions and conflicts within the charismatic movement as different cultural contexts and theological interpretations collide.

In summary, while charismatic doctrine is primarily shaped by biblical interpretation and spiritual experiences, it is also influenced by secular factors such as cultural trends, social movements, psychological factors, media and technology, consumer culture, and globalization. Understanding these secular influences can provide insight into the development, evolution, and diversity of charismatic theology and practice in contemporary Christianity.

Worship and Experience in the Charismatic Movement

Worship lies at the heart of the Charismatic Movement, serving as a central expression of devotion, intimacy with God, and spiritual encounter.

Charismatic worship is characterized by its vibrant, experiential nature, emphasizing the active presence of the Holy Spirit, the use of contemporary music and artistic expressions, and the freedom for spontaneous expressions of praise and worship.

This comprehensive exploration will delve into the various dimensions of worship and experience within the Charismatic Movement, including contemporary worship styles, the role of music and dance, and practices such as speaking in tongues and prophecy.

Contemporary Worship Styles

Charismatic worship is known for its contemporary and dynamic style, reflecting the cultural and musical preferences of the congregants. Unlike traditional forms of worship, which may involve hymns and liturgical elements, charismatic worship often incorporates modern music genres, such as rock, pop, gospel, and electronic dance music, to create an atmosphere of celebration, joy, and spiritual engagement.

Contemporary worship services typically feature live bands or praise teams leading congregational singing, accompanied by various instruments, including guitars, drums, keyboards, and percussion. Songs are selected for their theological content, emotional resonance, and ability to facilitate corporate worship, emphasizing heartfelt expression, authenticity, and participation from the congregation.

The structure of charismatic worship services may vary. Still, common elements often include times of praise and adoration, where believers express their love and gratitude to God through singing and dancing; times of worship and intimacy, where believers draw near to God in prayer, meditation, and reflection; and times of prophetic proclamation, where believers declare God's truth and purpose over their lives and circumstances.

Role of Music and Dance

Music plays a central role in charismatic worship, serving as a powerful medium for encountering the presence of God, expressing heartfelt devotion, and fostering unity and community among believers. Charismatic worship songs are characterized by their emotive lyrics, uplifting melodies, and repetitive choruses that invite participation and engagement from the congregation.

Worship songs often focus on themes such as God's love and faithfulness, the power of the cross, the victory of Christ, and the believer's identity and destiny in Christ. These songs are designed to evoke a range of emotions, from joy and celebration to reverence and awe, and to create an atmosphere conducive to spiritual encounter and transformation.

In addition to music, dance is another expressive form of worship commonly found in charismatic gatherings. Dance is viewed as a physical expression of praise and adoration, glorifying God with the body and engaging the whole person—body, soul, and spirit—in worship. Charismatic dancers often use movement, gestures, and choreography to convey spiritual truths, tell stories, and express the emotions and themes of worship songs.

The charismatic church has a unique relationship with entertainment, often incorporating music, drama, and multimedia elements into its worship services and events.

Here's how the charismatic church intersects with entertainment:

Dynamic Worship:

Worship is a central aspect of charismatic church services, and music plays a significant role in creating an atmosphere of praise and adoration. Charismatic worship often features contemporary Christian music with upbeat tempos, expressive lyrics, and emotional engagement. Musicians, singers, and worship leaders use their talents to lead congregants into a more profound experience of God's presence through music and song.

Creative Expression:

Charismatic churches value creative expression to engage with Scripture, share testimonies, and communicate spiritual truths. This can include dramatic presentations, skits, dance performances, and visual arts that convey biblical messages in innovative and engaging ways. These creative elements add variety and depth to worship services, appealing to individuals with different learning styles and preferences.

Media and Technology:

Charismatic churches often leverage media and technology to enhance their worship experiences and reach wider audiences. This may include using video projections, lighting effects, sound systems, and live streaming to create immersive environments and engage congregants visually and audibly. Multimedia presentations, testimonial videos, and live broadcasts enable charismatic churches to connect with believers beyond the physical confines of their church buildings.

Christian Entertainment Industry:

The charismatic movement has also contributed to the growth of the Christian entertainment industry, which produces music, films, books, and other media with a Christian message. Charismatic churches and ministries support and promote Christian artists, filmmakers, authors, and performers who share their values and beliefs. These collaborations help to cultivate a vibrant ecosystem of Christian entertainment that serves as an alternative to secular media.

Cultural Engagement:

Charismatic churches recognize the importance of engaging with popular culture and addressing contemporary issues through entertainment. Some charismatic leaders and ministries produce relevant content that speaks to the cultural context and resonates with younger generations. This can include addressing social justice issues, promoting positive values, and offering hope and inspiration through music, films, and other forms of entertainment.

Cautionary Notes:

While entertainment can be a powerful tool for engaging with audiences and conveying spiritual truths, charismatic churches also exercise caution to ensure that entertainment does not overshadow the central focus on worshiping God and proclaiming the gospel. There is a recognition that entertainment should serve as a means to an end—facilitating worship, edification, and evangelism—rather than becoming an end in itself.

In summary, the charismatic church embraces entertainment as a means of worship, creative expression, cultural engagement, and outreach. Charismatic churches seek to engage believers and seekers through dynamic worship, creative arts, multimedia presentations, and collaboration with the Christian entertainment industry, conveying the gospel's message in relevant and compelling ways.

The Charismatic Church and Music

The charismatic church has produced numerous talented musicians and singers who have significantly contributed to Christian music and worship.

These artists often blend contemporary Christian music, gospel, and worship music, creating a distinctive sound that resonates with believers worldwide.

Here are some of the most prominent bands and singers coming from the charismatic church:

Hillsong Worship:

Hillsong Worship is arguably one of the most well-known and influential worship bands to emerge from the charismatic movement. Originating from Hillsong Church in Sydney, Australia, the group has produced countless worship songs that have become staples in churches worldwide. With powerful anthems such as "Shout to the Lord," "Mighty to Save," and "Oceans (Where Feet May Fail)," Hillsong Worship has played a significant role in shaping the modern worship landscape.

Bethel Music:

Based out of Bethel Church in Redding, California, Bethel Music is another influential worship collective within the charismatic movement. Known for their passionate worship and prophetic songwriting, Bethel Music has released numerous albums featuring artists such as Brian and Jenn Johnson, Steffany Gretzinger, and Amanda Lindsey Cook. Songs like "No Longer Slaves," "Reckless Love," and "Raise a Hallelujah" have resonated deeply with believers worldwide.

Elevation Worship:

Elevation Worship, hailing from Elevation Church in Charlotte, North Carolina, has risen to prominence in the contemporary Christian music scene. Their anthemic worship songs, including "Do It Again," "Here as in Heaven," and "Graves into Gardens," have become favorites in churches globally. Elevation Worship's heartfelt lyrics and dynamic music have touched the hearts of believers seeking to encounter God's presence in worship.

Jesus Culture:

Originating from Bethel Church in Redding, California, Jesus Culture is a worship collective known for its passionate worship and commitment to encountering God's presence. Led by worship leaders such as Kim Walker-Smith, Chris Quilala, and Bryan and Katie Torwalt, Jesus Culture has released numerous albums featuring songs like "How He Loves," "Rooftops," and "Fierce" that have impacted the global worship community.

Planetshakers:

Hailing from Planetshakers Church in Melbourne, Australia, Planetshakers is a dynamic worship band known for their energetic live performances and uplifting praise music. Their albums feature songs like "The Anthem," "Nothing Is Impossible," and "Endless Praise," which are prevalent in charismatic and Pentecostal churches worldwide. Planetshakers' music reflects a heart for revival and a desire to see believers experience God's power and presence.

These are just a few examples of the many talented bands and singers that have emerged from the charismatic church.

Their music inspires, encourages, and uplifts believers worldwide, providing a soundtrack for worship and spiritual growth within the charismatic movement and beyond.

Practices such as Speaking in Tongues and Prophecy

In charismatic worship settings, speaking in tongues and prophecy are often valued as authentic expressions of the Holy Spirit's presence and activity among believers.

These practices are rooted in biblical accounts of spiritual gifts and manifestations of the Holy Spirit, particularly in the book of Acts and the Apostle Paul's writings.

Speaking in Tongues:

Speaking in tongues, or glossolalia, is speaking in a language unknown to the speaker, often accompanied by a sense of spiritual empowerment and anointing from the Holy Spirit. Charismatic Christians believe that speaking in tongues is a supernatural gift the Holy Spirit gives for prayer, praise, and edification (1 Corinthians 14:2). Tongues may be spoken individually or corporately. Believers are encouraged to pray for the interpretation of tongues so that the message may be understood and edifying to the church (1 Corinthians 14:13).

Prophecy:

Prophecy is the practice of speaking forth a message from God under the inspiration and guidance of the Holy Spirit. Charismatic Christians believe that prophecy is a gift of the Spirit given to believers for edification, exhortation, and comfort (1 Corinthians 14:3).

Prophetic messages may include encouragement, warnings, guidance, or revelation about God's plans and purposes. Prophecy is viewed as building up the body of Christ, strengthening believers' faith, and aligning individuals and communities with God's will.

In charismatic worship services, times of prophetic ministry may be incorporated into the worship flow, allowing believers to share words of prophecy, encouragement, or revelation as they are led by the Holy Spirit. Prophetic utterances may be spoken aloud, sung, or expressed through other creative means, such as art, poetry, or spontaneous worship.

Conclusion

In summary, worship and experience in the Charismatic Movement are characterized by their vibrant, expressive, and participatory nature, emphasizing the active presence of the Holy Spirit, the use of contemporary music and artistic expressions, and the freedom for spontaneous expressions of praise and worship.

Through contemporary worship styles, music and dance, and practices such as speaking in tongues and prophecy, charismatic believers seek to encounter God in a profound and transformative way, expressing their love, devotion, and adoration to Him and experiencing His presence and power in their midst.

As believers gather to worship, they are united in their pursuit of intimacy with God, their desire to exalt the name of Jesus, and their expectation of encountering the living God in their midst.

Community and Fellowship in the Charismatic Movement

Community and fellowship are foundational elements of the Charismatic Movement, providing believers with a sense of belonging, support, and spiritual growth within the church.

This comprehensive exploration will delve into community and fellowship within the Charismatic Movement, including small groups and cell churches, leadership structures, and accountability and discipleship practices.

Small Groups and Cell Churches

Small groups play a vital role in fostering community and fellowship within the Charismatic Movement, providing believers with opportunities for deeper relationships, mutual support, and spiritual growth. Small groups typically consist of a dozen members who meet regularly in homes, coffee shops, or other informal settings to study the Bible, pray, worship, and share life together.

Cell churches, a variation of small groups, are a common feature of charismatic churches, especially in larger congregations where the sense of intimacy and connection may be more challenging to maintain.

In a cell church model, the larger congregation is divided into smaller cell groups, each led by a trained facilitator or leader who oversees the members' spiritual growth and pastoral care.

Small groups and cell churches provide believers with a sense of community and belonging, allowing them to form deeper relationships with fellow believers, share their faith journey, and receive encouragement and support in times of need.

These groups also serve as a context for discipleship, accountability, and ministry training, empowering believers to grow in their faith and live out their calling as disciples of Christ.

Leadership Structures

Leadership structures within the Charismatic Movement vary widely depending on the size and context of the church or ministry organization. However, several everyday leadership roles and structures can be observed across charismatic churches and ministries:

Senior Pastor:

The senior pastor serves as the church's primary spiritual leader and visionary, providing the congregation direction, oversight, and pastoral care.

The senior pastor is often responsible for preaching, teaching, and casting vision for the church's mission and ministry.

Associate Pastors and Ministers:

Associate pastors and ministers assist the senior pastor in various areas of ministry, such as pastoral care, discipleship, worship, and outreach.

They may oversee specific ministries or departments within the church and work closely with the senior pastor to implement the church's vision and goals.

Elders and Deacons:

Elders and deacons serve as spiritual overseers and servant leaders within the church, providing guidance, support, and pastoral care to the congregation. Elders are responsible for the spiritual oversight and governance of the church. At the same time, deacons serve in practical areas of ministry, such as hospitality, outreach, and mercy ministry.

Small Group Leaders:

Small group leaders are crucial in facilitating community and discipleship within the church, leading small group meetings, facilitating discussions, and providing pastoral care and support to group members.

Ministry Leaders and Teams:

Ministry leaders oversee specific areas of ministry within the church, such as worship, youth, children, outreach, and missions. They recruit and train volunteers, coordinate ministry activities and events, and ensure the effective functioning of their respective ministries.

Prophetic and Apostolic Leaders:

In some charismatic churches and ministries, individuals may function in prophetic or apostolic roles, providing spiritual oversight, direction, and revelation to the church body. These leaders may operate in the gifts of prophecy, healing, and supernatural ministry, guiding the church in spiritual discernment and alignment with God's purposes.

Accountability and Discipleship

Accountability and discipleship are essential components of community life within the Charismatic Movement. They provide believers with the support, guidance, and encouragement they need to grow in their faith and walk with God. Charismatic churches and ministries employ various strategies and practices to promote accountability and discipleship among their members:

One-on-One Mentoring:

Many charismatic churches encourage believers to participate in one-on-one mentoring relationships with mature Christians who can provide spiritual guidance, support, and accountability. These mentoring relationships may involve regular meetings for Bible study, prayer, and personal sharing, as well as opportunities for discipleship and growth.

Small Group Discipleship:

Small groups serve as a context for discipleship and spiritual formation within the Charismatic Movement, providing believers with opportunities to study the Bible, pray, worship, and grow together in community. Small group leaders are crucial in facilitating discipleship and providing pastoral care and support to group members.

Accountability Partnerships:

Believers are encouraged to form accountability partnerships with fellow Christians who can provide support, encouragement, and accountability in spiritual growth and personal development.

Accountability partners meet regularly to share their struggles, victories, and prayer needs, holding each other accountable for living out their faith and following God's Word.

Leadership Oversight:

Charismatic churches and ministries typically have established leadership oversight and accountability structures to ensure the spiritual health and integrity of the church body. Senior pastors, elders, and other church leaders provide pastoral care, guidance, and oversight to members, addressing issues of doctrine, conduct, and pastoral concern as needed.

Training and Equipping:

Charismatic churches and ministries offer training and equipping programs to help believers grow in their understanding of the Bible, develop their spiritual gifts, and fulfill their God-given calling and destiny. These programs may include Bible studies, seminars, workshops, and conferences on discipleship, leadership, evangelism, and spiritual warfare.

Conclusion

In summary, community and fellowship are integral aspects of the Charismatic Movement, providing believers with a sense of belonging, support, and spiritual growth within the church context.

Charismatic Christians cultivate authentic relationships, receive spiritual guidance and support through small groups and cell churches, leadership structures, and practices such as accountability and discipleship, and are empowered to live out their faith and fulfill their calling as disciples of Christ.

As believers gather together in the community, they experience the transformative power of God's love, grace, and presence in their lives. They are strengthened and equipped to impact their families, communities, and the world for the glory of God.

Missions and Evangelism in the Charismatic Movement

Missions and evangelism are central aspects of the Charismatic Movement, reflecting its commitment to sharing the gospel, making disciples, and impacting communities and nations worldwide.

This comprehensive exploration will delve into the Charismatic Movement's global impact, evangelism strategies, and charismatic approaches to social justice and humanitarian aid.

Global Impact of the Charismatic Movement

The Charismatic Movement has profoundly impacted global Christianity, shaping the beliefs, practices, and expressions of faith in diverse cultural contexts and regions. Since its emergence in the early 20th century, the Charismatic Movement has grown exponentially, spreading to every continent and influencing millions of believers across denominational lines.

One of the hallmarks of the Charismatic Movement is its emphasis on empowering the Holy Spirit for ministry and mission. Charismatic Christians believe in the ongoing work of the Holy Spirit in the world, empowering believers to proclaim the gospel, demonstrate God's love and power, and make disciples of all nations (Matthew 28:19-20).

As a result, the Charismatic Movement has played a significant role in global missions and evangelism, with charismatic churches and ministries actively involved in outreach, church planting, and discipleship efforts in regions where Christianity is snowballing, as well as in areas where the gospel message has yet to be fully proclaimed.

Strategies for Evangelism

Charismatic churches and ministries employ various strategies and approaches to evangelism tailored to the cultural context and needs of the communities they seek to reach.

Some standard techniques for evangelism within the Charismatic Movement include:

Power Evangelism:

Charismatic Christians believe in the power of the Holy Spirit to accompany and confirm the preaching of the gospel with signs and wonders (Mark 16:20). Power evangelism involves praying for the sick, casting out demons, and demonstrating God's supernatural power as a means of authenticating the message of salvation and drawing people to faith in Christ.

Mass Crusades and Revival Meetings:

Charismatic evangelists often conduct mass crusades and revival meetings in cities and regions with spiritual hunger and openness to the gospel. These meetings feature dynamic preaching, passionate worship, and opportunities for personal response and prayer, leading to mass conversions and life transformations.

Charismatic Revival

In the charismatic church, revival is crucial as it embodies a spiritual awakening and renewal within the church and the broader community. Revival is often seen as intensified spiritual fervor, increased hunger for God, and a deepened sense of repentance and transformation. Here's an overview of the charismatic church's concept of revival:

Definition:

Revival in the charismatic church is understood as a sovereign move of the Holy Spirit, characterized by a widespread outpouring of God's presence and power. It is often marked by an increased emphasis on prayer, worship, repentance, and evangelism, leading to personal and corporate revival.

Historical Roots:

The charismatic concept of revival traces its roots to historical revival movements, such as the Great Awakenings in the United States and the Welsh Revival, where believers experienced profound encounters with God and witnessed widespread conversions and spiritual transformations.

Prayer and Intercession:

Prayer is central in preparing the way for revival in charismatic theology. Believers are encouraged to pray for spiritual breakthroughs, revival fire, and the manifestation of God's kingdom on earth. Intercessory prayer meetings and gatherings are often organized as a precursor to revival.

Worship and Praise:

Charismatic revival is closely associated with vibrant worship and passionate praise. Worship services during revival are characterized by heartfelt expressions of adoration, intimacy with God, and a hunger for His presence. Music, singing, and spontaneous worship are integral components of revival gatherings.

Signs and Wonders:

Miracles, healings, and supernatural manifestations are often prominent features of revival in the charismatic church. Believers expect to see God move in powerful ways, demonstrating His authority and transforming lives through miraculous interventions and divine encounters.

Repentance and Transformation:

Revival brings about a deep sense of conviction and repentance as individuals encounter the holiness and glory of God. It leads to a turning away from sin, a renewed commitment to righteousness, and a desire for personal and corporate transformation.

Evangelism and Outreach:

Charismatic revival is not confined to the four walls of the church. Still, it extends outward into the community through evangelism and outreach efforts. Believers are impassioned to share the gospel message, make disciples, and see lives transformed by the power of God.

Continual Seeking:

While revival may be experienced as a distinct season of heightened spiritual activity, the charismatic church emphasizes the importance of continually seeking God's presence and revival fire. Believers are encouraged to cultivate a lifestyle of prayer, worship, and spiritual hunger, remaining open to ongoing encounters with the Holy Spirit.

In essence, revival in the charismatic church is not merely an event but a spiritual awakening that ignites hearts, transforms lives, and ushers in God's kingdom purposes on earth. It is a divine invitation to encounter the living God in a profound and life-changing way.

Community Outreach and Service Projects:

Charismatic churches and ministries engage in community outreach and service projects to demonstrate God's love and compassion to those in need. These projects may include feeding programs, medical clinics, orphan care, and disaster relief efforts, providing practical assistance and spiritual support to individuals and families in crisis.

Prayer Walking and Spiritual Mapping:

Charismatic Christians engage in prayer walking and mapping to identify spiritual strongholds, areas of spiritual need, and opportunities for evangelism and ministry. By praying strategically and interceding for specific locations and people groups, believers seek to break spiritual barriers and see the gospel penetrate every sphere of society.

Media and Technology:

Charismatic churches and ministries utilize media and technology, such as radio, television, the internet, and social media, to reach a wider audience with the gospel message. Charismatic leaders and evangelists can share their messages and testimonies with people worldwide through online streaming, podcasts, and social media platforms, leading to salvation and spiritual awakenings.

Charismatic Approaches to Social Justice and Humanitarian Aid

In addition to evangelism, the Charismatic Movement is increasingly engaged in social justice and humanitarian aid efforts, reflecting its commitment to holistic ministry and the transformation of individuals and communities.

Charismatic Christians believe that the gospel encompasses spiritual and social dimensions, calling believers to address injustice, poverty, and oppression in the name of Christ.

Charismatic approaches to social justice and humanitarian aid include:

Advocacy and Awareness:

Charismatic churches and ministries advocate for social justice and raise awareness about human trafficking, poverty, racial reconciliation, and environmental stewardship. Through preaching, teaching, and public speaking, charismatic leaders challenge believers to act compassionately and advocate for the marginalized and oppressed.

Community Development:

Charismatic churches and ministries are involved in community development projects to empower individuals and communities to break the cycle of poverty and dependence. These projects may include vocational training, microenterprise development, education initiatives, and healthcare programs, providing practical assistance and empowering people to improve their quality of life.

Justice Ministries:

Charismatic Christians are involved in justice ministries that address systemic injustices and promote reconciliation and societal healing. These ministries may focus on racial reconciliation, criminal justice reform, immigration rights, and gender equality, advocating for policies and practices that reflect God's heart for justice and righteousness.

Humanitarian Aid:

Charismatic churches and ministries respond to humanitarian crises and disasters by providing emergency relief, food, shelter, and medical care to those in need. Charismatic Christians mobilize resources and volunteers through partnerships with local and international organizations to bring practical assistance and hope to people affected by conflict, natural disasters, and other humanitarian emergencies.

Conclusion

In summary, missions and evangelism are central aspects of the Charismatic Movement, reflecting its commitment to sharing the gospel, making disciples, and impacting communities and nations worldwide.

Charismatic Christians actively fulfill the Great Commission and demonstrate God's love and compassion to a hurting and broken world through strategies such as power evangelism, mass crusades, community outreach, media and technology, and social justice and humanitarian aid. As believers partner with the Holy Spirit in mission and ministry, they are empowered to proclaim the gospel boldly and demonstrate God's power supernaturally.

Challenges and Controversies in the Charismatic Movement

The Charismatic Movement, like any religious or spiritual movement, has faced its share of challenges and controversies throughout its history. These challenges have ranged from theological debates to ethical concerns, and they have shaped the development and direction of the movement in significant ways.

In this comprehensive exploration, we will delve into three key challenges and controversies within the Charismatic Movement:

- the Prosperity Gospel debate,
- issues of spiritual authority and accountability,
- and strategies for handling criticisms and skepticism.

The Prosperity Gospel Debate

One of the most hotly debated topics within the Charismatic Movement is the Prosperity Gospel, also known as the "health and wealth" or "name it and claim it" gospel.

This theological perspective teaches that God desires financial prosperity and physical well-being for all believers and that faith, positive confession, and financial giving are the keys to unlocking these blessings.

Proponents of the Prosperity Gospel argue that God wants His children to prosper in every area of life, including their finances, health, and relationships. They point to biblical promises of abundance and prosperity, such as Malachi 3:10 ("Bring the whole tithe into the storehouse, that there may be food in my house. Test me in this," says the Lord Almighty, "and see if I will not throw open the floodgates of heaven and pour out so much blessing that there will not be room enough to store it."), and John 10:10 ("The thief comes only to steal and kill and destroy; I have come that they may have life, and have it to the full.").

Critics of the Prosperity Gospel, however, argue that this theological perspective distorts the genuine message of the gospel and promotes materialism, greed, and spiritual manipulation. They point to the teachings of Jesus and the apostles, emphasizing the importance of humility, self-sacrifice, and eternal treasures over earthly riches (Matthew 6:19-21, Luke 6:20-26).

The Prosperity Gospel debate has sparked intense theological and ethical discussions within the Charismatic Movement, with some charismatic leaders and theologians distancing themselves from the Prosperity Gospel and advocating for a more balanced and biblically grounded approach to faith and finances.

Others continue to embrace and promote Prosperity Gospel teachings, leading to ongoing controversy and division within the movement.

Spiritual Authority and Accountability

Another challenge within the Charismatic Movement is the issue of spiritual authority and accountability, particularly concerning charismatic leaders and ministries. Charismatic churches and ministries are often led by dynamic and influential leaders who wield considerable spiritual authority and influence over their followers.

While spiritual authority can be a positive force for leadership, guidance, and pastoral care, it can also be susceptible to abuse, manipulation, and misuse. There have been numerous cases of charismatic leaders who have been accused of financial impropriety, sexual misconduct, authoritarianism, and other forms of abuse of power.

The lack of formal structures of accountability and oversight within many charismatic churches and ministries has contributed to a culture of secrecy and cover-up, making it difficult for victims to come forward and seek justice.

In recent years, the Charismatic Movement has grown awareness and concern about the need for greater transparency, accountability, and safeguards against abuse.

Some charismatic leaders and organizations have taken proactive steps to address these issues by implementing policies and procedures for preventing and responding to misconduct allegations, establishing independent oversight boards or councils, and providing training and resources on ethical leadership and pastoral care.

Handling Criticisms and Skepticism

Criticism and skepticism are inevitable aspects of any religious or spiritual movement, and the Charismatic Movement is no exception. Charismatic beliefs and practices, such as speaking in tongues, prophecy, and faith healing, have often been met with skepticism and criticism from both within and outside the church.

One challenge for charismatic believers is responding to criticisms and skepticism constructively and respectfully. While defending and articulating one's beliefs with confidence and conviction is crucial, engaging with skeptics and critics in a spirit of humility, openness, and dialogue is also essential.

Charismatic Christians can respond to criticisms and skepticism by:

Engaging in respectful dialogue:

Charismatic believers can engage with skeptics and critics in respectful dialogue, listening to their concerns and questions with empathy and understanding. Charismatic Christians can foster mutual respect and understanding by being willing to engage in conversation and address misconceptions or misunderstandings.

Providing evidence and testimonies:

Charismatic believers can share personal testimonies and examples of how their faith has impacted their lives and the lives of others. By providing tangible evidence of the transformative power of the Holy

Spirit, believers can help dispel misconceptions and demonstrate the validity of charismatic beliefs and experiences.

Maintaining humility and integrity:

Charismatic believers can respond to criticisms and skepticism with humility and integrity, acknowledging that they do not have all the answers and that their faith is ultimately a matter of personal conviction and experience. By embodying the values of humility, honesty, and authenticity, believers can model the character of Christ and attract others to the gospel message.

Practicing discernment and accountability:

Charismatic believers can exercise discernment and accountability in their beliefs and practices, carefully avoiding excesses, extremes, and abuses of spiritual power. By holding themselves and their leaders accountable to biblical standards of integrity and ethics, believers can maintain the credibility and witness of the Charismatic Movement.

Handling criticisms and skepticism is critical to being part of the charismatic church, as with any religious or spiritual movement.

Here are some critical strategies for effectively addressing criticisms and skepticism within the charismatic community:

Listen and Understand:

It's essential to listen carefully to the criticisms and concerns raised by others, including skeptics, both within and outside the charismatic church.

Seek to understand their perspectives and motivations for questioning certain beliefs or practices.

Demonstrating empathy and openness to dialogue can help foster mutual respect and understanding, even amid disagreements.

Engage with Humility:

Approach criticisms and skepticism with humility, recognizing that no individual or movement is immune to error or scrutiny. Humility involves acknowledging the limitations of human understanding and being open to correction and growth. Avoid becoming defensive or dismissive in response to criticisms, and instead, strive to engage in constructive dialogue with a spirit of humility and teachability.

Provide Biblical Support:

Providing biblical support for your beliefs and actions is vital when addressing criticisms of charismatic beliefs or practices. Charismatic theology is often grounded in scripture, and articulating the biblical basis for your beliefs can help alleviate concerns and clarify misunderstandings.

Point to relevant passages of scripture that support the charismatic emphasis on spiritual gifts, divine healing, and the work of the Holy Spirit.

Offer Personal Testimony:

Share your experiences and testimonies of how God has worked in your life through the charismatic church. Personal testimonies can be powerful tools for demonstrating the reality of God's presence, power, and transformational work.

By sharing your stories of spiritual encounters, answered prayers, and experiences of God's love and grace, you can provide tangible evidence of the validity and relevance of charismatic beliefs and practices.

Address Concerns Responsibly:

Take criticisms and skepticism seriously and address them responsibly within the charismatic community. This may involve conducting internal discussions, seeking input from knowledgeable leaders and theologians, and engaging in thoughtful reflection and study. Be willing to reevaluate beliefs and practices in light of constructive feedback and new insights while remaining rooted in the foundational truths of the Christian faith.

Model Love and Unity:

Above all, strive to model love, grace, and unity in your interactions with others, both within and outside the charismatic church.

Remember that we are called to love one another as Christ has loved us, even when we disagree or hold different perspectives.

By demonstrating Christ-like love and unity, we can effectively counter criticisms and skepticism and witness the gospel's transformative power in our lives and communities.

In conclusion, the Charismatic Movement faces various challenges and controversies, including debates over the Prosperity Gospel, spiritual authority and accountability issues, and criticisms and skepticism from both within and outside the church.

While these challenges are significant, they also present opportunities for growth, reflection, and reform within the movement.

By engaging in constructive dialogue, promoting transparency and accountability, and responding with humility and integrity, charismatic believers can navigate these challenges with grace and wisdom, ultimately strengthening the witness and impact of the Charismatic Movement in the world.

Charismatic Spirituality in Everyday Life

Charismatic spirituality permeates every aspect of believers' lives, shaping their prayer and devotional practices, understanding spiritual warfare, and pursuing personal growth and transformation.

This exploration will explore how charismatic spirituality influences everyday life, focusing on prayer and devotional life, spiritual warfare, and personal growth and transformation.

Prayer and Devotional Life

Prayer lies at the heart of charismatic spirituality, serving as a vital means of communion with God, a channel for receiving guidance and revelation from the Holy Spirit, and a catalyst for spiritual breakthrough and transformation. Charismatic believers approach prayer with a sense of expectancy and faith, believing God hears and answers their prayers according to His will and purposes.

Charismatic prayer is characterized by its spontaneity, fervency, and reliance on the leading of the Holy Spirit. Believers are encouraged to pray in the Spirit, allowing the Holy Spirit to intercede through them with groans that cannot be expressed in words (Romans 8:26).

This may involve praying in tongues, a spiritual language the Holy Spirit gives for edification and intercession (1 Corinthians 14:2).

In addition to praying in tongues, charismatic believers engage in various practices, including intercessory prayer, petitionary prayer, thanksgiving, and worship.

They pray with boldness and confidence, knowing that they have access to the throne of grace through Jesus Christ (Hebrews 4:16) and that their prayers can effect change in their lives and the world around them.

Devotional life is also central to charismatic spirituality, as believers seek to cultivate intimacy with God through regular Bible reading, meditation, and reflection. Charismatic believers are encouraged to approach the Scriptures with openness to the leading of the Holy

Spirit, allowing Him to illuminate the Word and reveal its deeper truths and applications to their lives.

Spiritual Warfare

Charismatic spirituality acknowledges the reality of spiritual warfare, the ongoing struggle between the forces of good and evil in the spiritual realm. Believers are taught to be vigilant and discerning, recognizing they are in a spiritual battle against spiritual powers and principalities (Ephesians 6:12).

Spiritual warfare takes many forms within charismatic spirituality, including prayer, fasting, proclaiming God's Word, and using spiritual gifts such as discernment, prophecy, and deliverance. Believers are equipped with spiritual armor (Ephesians 6:13-17), including the belt of truth, the breastplate of righteousness, the shoes of peace, the shield of faith, the helmet of salvation, and the sword of the Spirit, the Word of God.

Charismatic believers are taught to resist the devil and his schemes, standing firm in their faith and wielding the weapons of spiritual warfare to overcome the enemy's attacks and advance God's kingdom. They engage in spiritual battles not with physical weapons but with the power of prayer, the authority of God's Word, and the anointing of the Holy Spirit.

Personal Growth and Transformation

Personal growth and transformation are central goals of charismatic spirituality, as believers seek to become more like Christ in character, attitude, and behavior. Charismatic spirituality emphasizes the work of the Holy Spirit in sanctifying and empowering believers to live holy and victorious lives.

Charismatic believers are taught to pursue personal growth and transformation through various spiritual disciplines, including prayer, fasting, Bible study, worship, fellowship, and service. They recognize that spiritual growth is a lifelong process that requires intentional effort, dependence on the Holy Spirit, and participation in the life of the church community.

Being filled with the Holy Spirit is foundational to charismatic spirituality, as believers seek to experience God's presence and power. They believe the Holy Spirit empowers them to overcome sin, walk in obedience to God's Word, and bear fruit of the Spirit, such as love, joy, peace, patience, kindness, goodness, faithfulness, gentleness, and self-control (Galatians 5:22-23).

Charismatic spirituality also emphasizes the importance of spiritual gifts and ministries in the life of the believer and the church.

Believers are encouraged to discover, develop, and deploy their spiritual gifts to edify the body of Christ and advance God's kingdom. They are taught to operate in the power and anointing of the Holy Spirit, exercising discernment, faith, and love as they minister to others in Jesus' name.

In conclusion, charismatic spirituality permeates every aspect of believers' lives, shaping their prayer and devotional practices, their understanding of spiritual warfare, and pursuit of personal growth and transformation.

Through prayer and devotional life, believers cultivate intimacy with God and receive guidance and revelation from the Holy Spirit.

Through spiritual warfare, believers engage in the ongoing struggle against spiritual powers and principalities, wielding the weapons of prayer, faith, and the Word of God.

Through personal growth and transformation, believers are empowered by the Holy Spirit to become more like Christ in character, attitude, and behavior, bearing fruit of the Spirit and ministering in the power and anointing of the Holy Spirit for the glory of God.

Engaging with Culture and Society in the Charismatic Movement

Charismatic Christianity, emphasizing the power and presence of the Holy Spirit, has significantly shaped cultural and societal trends in the 21st century. In this exploration, we'll delve into how the Charismatic Movement engages with culture and society, focusing on its influence in media and the arts, its approach to political engagement and social issues, and the relevance of charismatic Christianity in the modern era.

Charismatic Influence in Media and Arts

The Charismatic Movement has profoundly impacted media and the arts, influencing everything from music and literature to film and television. Charismatic Christians have been at the forefront of producing and promoting music that reflects their faith and experiences, with genres such as contemporary Christian music (CCM), gospel, and worship music gaining widespread popularity.

Musicians and artists within the Charismatic Movement have used their talents and platforms to express their beliefs, share their testimonies, and inspire others in their faith journey. Artists like Hillsong Worship, Bethel Music, and Jesus Culture have gained international acclaim for their powerful worship anthems resonating with believers worldwide.

In addition to music, charismatic Christians have also made significant contributions to other forms of media and arts, including literature, film, and visual arts. Charismatic authors have written bestselling books on faith, healing, prophecy, and spiritual warfare. At the same time, filmmakers have produced movies and documentaries that explore themes of faith, redemption, and the supernatural.

Charismatic influence in media and arts extends beyond traditional forms of expression, including digital media and online platforms. Charismatic leaders and ministries have embraced social media, podcasts, and streaming platforms to reach a wider audience with their message and ministry, leveraging the power of technology to spread the gospel and build community in new and innovative ways.

Political Engagement and Social Issues

The Charismatic Movement has been actively engaged in political and social issues, advocating for justice, compassion, and righteousness in society. While charismatic Christians come from diverse political backgrounds and perspectives, they share a joint commitment to biblical values and principles that inform their approach to politics and social activism.

Charismatic Christians are often involved in grassroots movements and initiatives that seek to address issues such as poverty, inequality, racism, and human trafficking. They advocate for policies and practices that uphold human dignity, protect the vulnerable, and promote the common good, drawing inspiration from biblical teachings on justice, mercy, and compassion.

While some charismatic Christians engage in direct political action and advocacy, others focus on building relationships and bridges across political divides, seeking to be agents of reconciliation and healing in a polarized and divided society. They believe in the power of prayer, unity, and collective action to bring about positive change and transformation in their communities and nations.

Relevance of Charismatic Christianity in the 21st Century

In an increasingly secular and skeptical culture, charismatic Christianity remains relevant and vibrant, offering a dynamic and experiential faith that resonates with many people's spiritual hunger and longing in the modern era.

Charismatic Christianity provides a sense of belonging, purpose, and spiritual vitality often missing in secular society, drawing people into authentic encounters with God's presence and power.

One of the key factors driving the relevance of charismatic Christianity in the 21st century is its ability to adapt and innovate in response to changing cultural and societal trends. Charismatic churches and ministries embrace contemporary worship styles, digital media, and cultural relevance to connect with a new generation of believers and seekers, offering fresh expressions of faith that speak to the realities of life in the 21st century.

Another factor contributing to the relevance of charismatic Christianity is its emphasis on personal experience and encounter with the Holy Spirit. In an age of skepticism and uncertainty, charismatic Christians offer hope, healing, and transformation through encounters with the living God, who is actively at work in the world today. Charismatic spirituality provides a framework for experiencing God's presence and power in everyday life, empowering believers to live with faith, boldness, and purpose.

In conclusion, the Charismatic Movement engages with culture and society in diverse and dynamic ways, influencing media and the arts, advocating for justice and compassion, and offering a relevant and vibrant expression of faith in the 21st century.

Charismatic Christianity remains relevant and impactful, offering a message of hope, healing, and transformation that resonates with many people's spiritual hunger and longing in the modern era.

As charismatic Christians continue to engage with culture and society, they seek to be salt and light in a world hungry for the gospel's transformative power.

Unity and Diversity in the Charismatic Movement

Unity and diversity are fundamental aspects of the Charismatic Movement, which spans a wide range of theological traditions, cultural contexts, and denominational affiliations.

This exploration will delve into the ecumenical relations with other Christian traditions, the diversity within the Charismatic Movement, and the importance of building bridges across denominations.

Ecumenical Relations with Other Christian Traditions

The Charismatic Movement has significantly fostered ecumenical relations and dialogue among various Christian traditions, including Protestant, Catholic, Orthodox, and Pentecostal churches.

Despite theological differences and historical divisions, charismatic Christians recognize the common bond of faith in Jesus Christ and the shared experience of the Holy Spirit's presence and power.

Ecumenical gatherings, conferences, and events allow charismatic Christians from different traditions to unite in worship, prayer, and fellowship, celebrating their unity in Christ and seeking common ground for cooperation and collaboration in ministry and mission. These gatherings often feature ecumenical speakers, worship leaders, and participants who represent the diversity of the global church.

Charismatic leaders and organizations also engage in ecumenical initiatives and partnerships that promote unity, reconciliation, and cooperation across denominational lines.

These initiatives may include joint prayer initiatives, interchurch worship services, theological dialogues, and collaborative ministry projects that address the church's shared challenges and opportunities today.

While ecumenical relations within the Charismatic Movement are characterized by a spirit of openness, dialogue, and mutual respect, they also require humility, patience, and a willingness to listen and learn from one another. Charismatic Christians recognize that unity does not mean uniformity and that diversity enriches the body of Christ, reflecting the multifaceted nature of God's kingdom.

Diversity within the Charismatic Movement

The Charismatic Movement is characterized by its diversity, encompassing many theological perspectives, worship styles, cultural expressions, and denominational affiliations. Within the Charismatic Movement, believers may identify with different theological traditions, such as evangelical, Pentecostal, or mainline Protestant, each with distinct emphases and practices.

Worship styles within the Charismatic Movement vary widely, from traditional hymns and liturgies to contemporary praise and worship songs, reflecting the cultural and contextual diversity of charismatic churches and ministries worldwide. Some charismatic churches embrace a more spontaneous and informal approach to worship, with freedom for prophetic utterances, spiritual gifts, and expressions of joy and celebration.

Cultural diversity is also evident within the Charismatic Movement, as believers from different ethnic, racial, and linguistic backgrounds bring their unique cultural heritage and expressions of faith to the worshiping community.

Charismatic churches and ministries may incorporate indigenous culture, music, dance, and language elements into their worship services, creating a rich tapestry of diversity and unity in Christ.

Denominational diversity is another hallmark of the Charismatic Movement, with believers from various Christian traditions and denominations participating in charismatic renewal and expression. Charismatic Catholics, Orthodox, and mainline Protestants increasingly embrace charismatic spirituality. In contrast, charismatic Pentecostals and evangelical Christians continue to play a prominent role in the movement.

Building Bridges Across Denominations

Building bridges across denominations is essential for promoting unity, understanding, and cooperation within the Charismatic Movement and the broader body of Christ. Charismatic Christians are called to embody the unity of the Spirit in the bond of peace (Ephesians 4:3), transcending denominational differences and divisions to focus on their shared identity as followers of Jesus Christ.

Charismatic Christians build bridges across denominations through interchurch collaboration and partnership in ministry and mission.

Charismatic churches and ministries often work together on joint initiatives, such as community outreach, evangelistic campaigns, and social justice projects, pooling their resources and talents for the greater good of the kingdom.

Another way that charismatic Christians build bridges across denominations is through theological dialogue and engagement with other Christian traditions. Charismatic theologians and scholars participate in ecumenical forums, conferences, and publications that promote mutual understanding, theological exchange, and cooperation in areas of common concern and interest.

Charismatic Christians also build bridges across denominations through intentional efforts to foster relationships and friendships with believers from different traditions.

They seek opportunities for fellowship, prayer, and collaboration with brothers and sisters in Christ, recognizing that they have much to learn from one another and that their diversity enriches the body of Christ.

In conclusion, unity and diversity are fundamental aspects of the Charismatic Movement, which seeks to embrace the richness and complexity of the global body of Christ.

Through ecumenical relations with other Christian traditions, appreciation for diversity within the Charismatic Movement, and building bridges across denominations, charismatic Christians strive to embody the unity of the Spirit in the bond of peace, reflecting the diversity and unity of God's kingdom in the world.

Looking Ahead: Future Trends and Possibilities in the Charismatic Movement

As the Charismatic Movement continues to evolve and grow in the 21st century, it faces new opportunities and challenges in adapting to technological innovations, emerging global centers of charismatic Christianity, and changing cultural and generational shifts.

In this exploration, we'll delve into these future trends and possibilities, considering how the Charismatic Movement can navigate the opportunities and challenges of the future.

Technological Innovations in Ministry

Technological innovations have transformed every aspect of modern life, including how we communicate, learn, work, and worship. In the Charismatic Movement, technological advancements offer new opportunities for ministry and outreach, enabling charismatic churches and ministries to reach a wider audience, engage with believers innovatively, and deepen discipleship and spiritual growth.

One significant trend in technological innovations in ministry is the use of digital media and online platforms for worship, teaching, and community building. Charismatic churches and ministries increasingly leverage social media, live streaming, podcasts, and mobile apps to connect with believers, share sermons and teachings, and facilitate virtual small groups and discipleship programs.

Another trend is the development of immersive and interactive technologies, such as virtual reality (VR) and augmented reality (AR), to enhance the worship experience and facilitate spiritual encounters. Charismatic churches and ministries are exploring how VR and AR technologies can create immersive worship environments, interactive prayer experiences, and virtual pilgrimage sites that engage the senses and deepen spiritual engagement.

Artificial intelligence (AI) and machine learning can also enhance ministry effectiveness and efficiency, from personalized content recommendations and chatbots for pastoral care to data analytics for understanding trends and patterns in ministry engagement.

Charismatic churches and ministries are exploring how AI and machine learning can help them better understand and serve their congregations and communities.

Emerging Global Centers of Charismatic Christianity

The Charismatic Movement has experienced explosive growth and expansion in the global South, particularly in regions such as Africa, Latin America, and Asia, where charismatic Christianity thrives and significantly influences culture, society, and politics. These emerging global centers of charismatic Christianity represent new frontiers for ministry and mission, offering opportunities for cross-cultural collaboration, exchange, and partnership.

Africa, in particular, has emerged as a significant center of charismatic Christianity, with vibrant and dynamic charismatic churches and ministries transforming communities and nations. Charismatic leaders and churches in Africa are known for their emphasis on spiritual power, healing, deliverance, and social transformation, drawing believers from diverse backgrounds and denominational affiliations.

Latin America is another region where charismatic Christianity is experiencing rapid growth and expansion, fueled by a deep spiritual hunger and a desire for a personal encounter with God's presence and power. Charismatic churches and ministries in Latin America are known for their passionate worship, vibrant spirituality, and commitment to social justice and holistic ministry.

Asia is also witnessing a surge in charismatic Christianity, with charismatic churches and ministries proliferating across the region and attracting large numbers of believers, particularly among the younger generation. Charismatic leaders and churches in Asia are harnessing the power of digital media, youth engagement, and social entrepreneurship to advance the gospel and impact their communities for Christ.

Adapting to Changing Cultural and Generational Shifts

As cultural and generational shifts continue to reshape society and the church, the Charismatic Movement faces the challenge of adapting to changing demographics, preferences, and priorities while remaining faithful to its core beliefs and values. Charismatic churches and ministries must be nimble and flexible in responding to these shifts, seeking creative and innovative ways to engage with believers and seekers in a rapidly changing world.

One critical cultural shift is the growing influence of postmodernism and secularism, which challenge traditional notions of truth, authority, and spirituality. Charismatic churches and ministries must navigate the tension between embracing cultural relevance and remaining rooted in biblical truth, seeking to communicate the timeless message of the gospel in ways that resonate with contemporary culture.

Another generational shift is the rise of the millennial and Gen Z generations, who bring their unique perspectives, values, and preferences to the church. Charismatic churches and ministries must engage with millennials and Gen Z meaningfully, addressing their spiritual questions and concerns and providing opportunities for authentic community, discipleship, and mission.

Charismatic churches and ministries must also grapple with social justice, diversity, and inclusion issues as they seek to reflect the kingdom of God in a diverse and multicultural world. Charismatic leaders and churches must confront issues of racism, sexism, and injustice within their own communities and work toward greater diversity, equity, and reconciliation in the body of Christ.

In conclusion, the Charismatic Movement's future is filled with opportunities and challenges, from harnessing technological innovations for ministry to engaging with emerging global centers of charismatic Christianity and adapting to changing cultural and generational shifts.

Charismatic churches and ministries must remain faithful to their calling to proclaim the gospel and make disciples of all nations, seeking to embody God's love, power, and presence in a rapidly changing world.

By embracing creativity, innovation, and collaboration, the Charismatic Movement can continue to impact lives and transform communities for the glory of God.

Embracing the Charismatic Journey

As we conclude our exploration of the Charismatic Movement, it's essential to reflect on our journey, consider the personal growth and spiritual formation experienced along the way, and offer encouragement for the future of Charismatic Christianity.

The Charismatic Movement is more than a theological tradition or a set of practices; it's a dynamic and transformative journey of encountering the living God and experiencing the power of the Holy Spirit in our lives and communities.

Reflections on Personal Growth and Spiritual Formation

The Charismatic Journey is marked by personal growth and spiritual formation as believers respond to the call of the Holy Spirit to deeper intimacy with God, greater maturity in faith, and more effective ministry and service.

Along the journey, we've experienced moments of encounter with God's presence and power, conviction and transformation, and joy and celebration as we've witnessed God at work in our lives and communities.

One of the hallmarks of the Charismatic Journey is the emphasis on personal encounters with the Holy Spirit, who empowers us to live the Christian life with boldness, faith, and love.

Through prayer, worship, and studying God's Word, we've cultivated intimacy with God and grown in understanding His character, His will, and His purposes for our lives.

The Charismatic Journey is also characterized by spiritual gifts and ministries that build up the body of Christ and advance God's kingdom in the world. As we've embraced our spiritual gifts and exercised them in service to others, we've experienced the joy of seeing lives transformed, relationships restored, and communities impacted by the power of the gospel.

Encouragement for the Future of Charismatic Christianity

As we look to the future of Charismatic Christianity, we do so with hope and anticipation, knowing that the same Holy Spirit who has guided us on our journey thus far will continue to lead and empower us for the challenges and opportunities.

The Charismatic Movement is a living and dynamic expression of the church, continually adapting and evolving to meet the needs of believers and seekers in every generation and context.

We are encouraged by the continued growth and expansion of the Charismatic Movement in regions worldwide, particularly in the global South, where vibrant and dynamic charismatic churches and ministries transform communities and nations with the power of the gospel. We are inspired by the creativity, innovation, and passion of charismatic leaders and believers who are pioneering new ways of worship, ministry, and mission in response to the leading of the Holy Spirit.

We are also encouraged by the growing recognition of the importance of unity and diversity within the Charismatic Movement, as believers from different traditions, cultures, and denominations come together in worship, fellowship, and ministry, celebrating their shared faith in Jesus Christ and their everyday experience of the Holy Spirit's presence and power.

As we embrace the Charismatic Journey, let us do so with humility, openness, and a willingness to be led by the Holy Spirit into deeper intimacy with God, greater maturity in faith, and more effective ministry and service. Let us cultivate a culture of prayer, worship, and discipleship that empowers believers to live out their faith with passion, purpose, and boldness.

In conclusion, the Charismatic Movement is a journey of encounter with the living God and experiencing the power of the Holy Spirit in our lives and communities. As we reflect on our personal growth and spiritual formation along the way and offer encouragement for the future of Charismatic Christianity, let us do so with faith, hope, and love, knowing that God is faithful and that His Spirit will continue to lead and guide us on the journey ahead.

The Charismatic Movement in Africa

The Charismatic movement has significantly impacted Christianity in Africa, shaping its spirituality, worship practices, and community engagement.

Here are some key points about the charismatic church in Africa:

Rapid Growth:

The Charismatic movement has experienced exponential growth across Africa since the mid-20th century. It has become one of the most dominant expressions of Christianity in many African countries.

Emphasis on Spiritual Experience:

Charismatic churches in Africa strongly focus on the experiential aspects of Christianity, including speaking in tongues, healing, prophecy, and deliverance. These manifestations of the Holy Spirit are often central to their worship services and gatherings.

Role of Pentecostalism:

Pentecostalism, emphasizing the baptism of the Holy Spirit and the gifts of the Spirit, has been a driving force behind the growth of the charismatic movement in Africa. Many African charismatic churches identify as Pentecostal or have been influenced by Pentecostal theology and practices.

Indigenous Contextualization:

African charismatic churches often integrate indigenous cultural elements into their worship and ministry. This includes incorporating traditional music, dance, and spiritual practices into their services, creating a unique blend of spirituality that resonates with local communities.

Social Engagement:

Charismatic African churches are actively involved in social outreach and community development initiatives. They often run schools, orphanages, healthcare clinics, and vocational training centers to address the practical needs of their congregations and surrounding communities.

Leadership and Authority:

Charismatic churches in Africa are typically led by charismatic and often entrepreneurial leaders who hold significant authority within their congregations. These leaders are seen as spiritual fathers or mothers who guide, protect, and bless their followers.

Challenges and Controversies:

The charismatic movement in Africa is not without its challenges and controversies. Issues such as financial exploitation, moral scandals, and theological disagreements have surfaced within some charismatic churches, leading to criticisms from both within and outside the movement.

Global Influence:

Charismatic churches have increasingly become influential players in global Christianity. Many African charismatic leaders have gained international recognition and established networks with churches and ministries worldwide, contributing to the global spread of charismatic Christianity.

Overall, the charismatic church in Africa represents a dynamic and vibrant expression of Christianity that continues to shape the spiritual landscape of the continent and beyond.

Some common pros and cons associated with the charismatic church:

Pros:

Emphasis on Spiritual Experience:

Charismatic churches prioritize the experiential aspect of faith, encouraging members to encounter God through practices such as speaking in tongues, prophecy, and healing. This leads to a deeper spiritual connection for many believers.

Dynamic Worship:

Charismatic worship services are often characterized by vibrant music, passionate singing, and spontaneous expressions of praise and worship, creating an atmosphere of spiritual fervor and excitement.

Community and Fellowship:

Charismatic churches strongly emphasize building tight-knit communities where members support and encourage one another, fostering a sense of belonging and camaraderie among believers.

Mission and Evangelism:

Charismatic churches are often involved in evangelistic efforts, both locally and globally, spreading the message of Jesus Christ and making disciples through various outreach programs and mission initiatives.

Healing and Deliverance:

Many charismatic churches believe in divine healing and deliverance from spiritual oppression, offering prayer and ministry for physical, emotional, and spiritual restoration to those in need.

Charismatic Leadership:

Charismatic leaders are often seen as dynamic and visionary figures who inspire and motivate their followers, leading to personal growth, empowerment, and spiritual renewal among congregation members.

Cons:

Theological Controversies:

Charismatic churches may face theological controversies and disagreements, particularly around teachings related to spiritual gifts, prosperity theology, and the role of supernatural manifestations in the church, leading to divisions and doctrinal disputes.

Financial Exploitation:

Some charismatic leaders have been accused of financial exploitation, manipulation, and misuse of funds, raising concerns about transparency, accountability, and stewardship within specific charismatic ministries.

Emotionalism and Excesses:

The emphasis on emotional experiences and dramatic manifestations of the Holy Spirit in charismatic worship services can sometimes lead to emotionalism, sensationalism, and a focus on outward displays of spirituality rather than genuine spiritual maturity and discipleship.

Lack of Discernment:

In some charismatic circles, there may be a lack of discernment and critical thinking regarding spiritual experiences and supernatural phenomena, leaving believers vulnerable to deception, false teachings, and spiritual manipulation.

Cultural Insensitivity:

Charismatic churches that do not adequately contextualize their ministry within the cultural and social realities of their congregations and communities may inadvertently perpetuate cultural insensitivity, alienating certain groups and hindering effective communication of the gospel message.

Exclusivism and Division:

Charismatic churches that emphasize particular spiritual experiences or doctrinal beliefs as evidence of true faith may foster a sense of exclusivism and division within the broader body of Christ, leading to sectarianism and isolationism rather than unity and collaboration.

Modern Charismatic Leaders in Africa

In the modern-day African charismatic church, several central figures have emerged as influential leaders who have played significant roles in shaping the movement and impacting the spiritual landscape of the continent.

Here are some of the central figures:

Benson Idahosa (1938-1998):

Often referred to as the father of Pentecostalism in Nigeria, Benson Idahosa was a pioneering charismatic preacher and founder of the Church of God Mission International. He was known for his dynamic preaching, emphasis on faith, and belief in the power of the Holy Spirit to bring about miracles and signs.

Idahosa's ministry had a profound impact in Nigeria and across Africa and beyond, inspiring a new generation of charismatic leaders and churches.

David Oyedepo:

Founder and presiding bishop of the Living Faith Church Worldwide, also known as Winners' Chapel, David Oyedepo is one of Africa's most prominent charismatic leaders. His ministry, characterized by a strong emphasis on prosperity theology, faith, and divine healing, has grown into one of the largest Christian denominations in Nigeria and has branches in several other countries.

E. A. Adeboye:

Enoch Adejare Adeboye, commonly known as Pastor Adeboye, is the General Overseer of the Redeemed Christian Church of God (RCCG), one of the fastest-growing Pentecostal denominations in Nigeria and globally. Under his leadership, RCCG has experienced exponential growth and has become a significant force in the charismatic movement, with millions of members worldwide.

Chris Oyakhilome:

Founder and president of Believers' Love World Incorporated, Christ Embassy, Chris Oyakhilome is a charismatic preacher, teacher, and healing evangelist based in Nigeria. His ministry, characterized by a focus on the supernatural, divine healing, and the power of faith, has attracted millions of followers both in Africa and around the world through television and online platforms.

T. B. Joshua (1963-2021):

Temitope Balogun Joshua, commonly known as T. B. Joshua, was a Nigerian charismatic pastor, televangelist, and founder of the Synagogue, Church of All Nations (SCOAN). Known for his prophetic ministry, healing miracles, and humanitarian work, Joshua significantly influenced the charismatic movement in Africa and beyond until his passing in 2021.

Samuel Kakande:

Samuel Kakande, a Ugandan pastor and founder of the Synagogue Church of All Nations (SCOAN) in Uganda, has gained prominence for his healing ministry and prophetic gifts. His church, affiliated with the Nigerian SCOAN founded by T. B. Joshua, has attracted followers from Uganda and neighboring countries, making him one of the influential figures in the East African charismatic movement.

Shepherd Bushiri, also known as "Major 1," is a Malawian charismatic preacher, self-proclaimed prophet, and leader of the Enlightened Christian Gathering (ECG) church. He gained international prominence for his charismatic preaching style, claims of performing miracles, and flamboyant lifestyle.

Here's an overview of Shepherd Bushiri and his ministry:

Early Life and Ministry Beginnings:

Shepherd Bushiri was born on February 20, 1983, in Lilongwe, Malawi. He reportedly had a spiritual encounter at a young age and began his ministry as a preacher and evangelist. He later founded the Enlightened Christian Gathering (ECG) church, which multiplied in popularity, attracting thousands of followers in Malawi and beyond.

Teaching and Beliefs:

Bushiri's ministry is characterized by charismatic and prosperity gospel teachings. He emphasizes the power of faith, prayer, and positive confession to bring about blessings, breakthroughs, and miracles in the lives of believers.

Bushiri often preaches financial prosperity, divine healing, and spiritual warfare, promising supernatural interventions for those who adhere to his teachings and sowing financial seeds into his ministry.

Miracle Claims and Controversies:

Shepherd Bushiri has made numerous claims of performing miracles, including healings, deliverances, and prophetic revelations. He has been known to conduct large-scale "miracle crusades" and healing services, where attendees report experiencing supernatural manifestations and encounters. However, these claims have also sparked controversy and skepticism, with some critics accusing Bushiri of stage-managing miracles and exploiting vulnerable believers for financial gain.

Legal Troubles and Scandals:

Despite his popularity, Shepherd Bushiri has faced legal troubles and scandals throughout his career. In 2018, he was arrested in South Africa for fraud, money laundering, and organized crime related to his investment schemes. Bushiri and his wife, Mary, were also arrested in 2020 on charges of fraud and money laundering related to an investment scheme that allegedly defrauded thousands of people. In addition to his legal troubles, Bushiri has faced criticism for his opulent lifestyle, which includes luxury cars, private jets, and extravagant fashion.

Global Influence and Criticism:

Despite the controversies surrounding him, Shepherd Bushiri has maintained a significant following in Africa and internationally. His ministry has expanded to include branches in various countries, and he has a large following on social media platforms. However, Bushiri has also faced criticism from fellow Christian leaders, theologians, and watchdog groups who question the legitimacy of his claims, theology, and ethical conduct.

In summary, Shepherd Bushiri is a charismatic preacher and leader of the Enlightened Christian Gathering (ECG) church, known for his claims of performing miracles, teaching prosperity gospels, and having a controversial lifestyle.

While he has a considerable following and international influence, Bushiri has also faced legal troubles, scandals, and criticism from within the Christian community and beyond. His ministry highlights the complexities and controversies surrounding charismatic leaders and the prosperity gospel movement.

These central figures, among others, have played pivotal roles in shaping the modern-day African charismatic church, contributing to its growth, influence, and impact on the continent's spiritual, social, and cultural landscape.

The Concept Of Faith

In the charismatic church, the concept of faith holds a central and foundational role in both theology and practice. Faith is not merely an intellectual assent to doctrinal beliefs but a dynamic and transformative force that empowers believers to experience the reality of God's kingdom in their lives.

Here's an overview of the charismatic church's concept of faith:

Definition:

In the charismatic tradition, faith is understood as complete trust, confidence, and reliance on God and His promises. It is believing in the unseen and trusting in the character and faithfulness of God, even in the face of uncertainty and adversity.

Scriptural Basis:

Charismatic theology emphasizes the biblical teaching of faith, drawing inspiration from passages such as Hebrews 11:1, which defines faith as "the assurance of things hoped for, the conviction of things not seen." The charismatic church views faith as a gift from God and a vital aspect of the believer's relationship with Him.

Active and Living:

Charismatic faith is not passive but active and dynamic. It involves obeying God's word, taking risks, and boldly pursuing His purposes. Faith is demonstrated through action as believers step into the supernatural realm and expect God to intervene miraculously.

Confession and Declaration:

In the charismatic church, faith is often expressed through confession and declaration of God's promises. Believers are encouraged to speak words of faith and agreement with Scripture, declaring God's truth over their lives and circumstances, even when faced with challenges or obstacles.

Healing and Miracles:

Charismatic theology strongly emphasizes the power of faith to bring about healing and miracles. Believers are taught to pray with faith for physical, emotional, and spiritual restoration, expecting God to intervene supernaturally according to His will.

Prosperity Theology:

Some segments of the charismatic church subscribe to prosperity theology, which teaches that faith is the key to material and financial blessings. According to this belief, prosperity, and success are evidence of strong faith, leading to an emphasis on positive confession, sowing seeds of faith, and expecting material abundance.

Testing and Growth:

Charismatic faith is often tested and refined through trials, challenges, and experiences of adversity. Believers are encouraged to persevere, trusting God's faithfulness and sovereignty, even when circumstances seem bleak or uncertain.

Personal Relationship:

Ultimately, faith in the charismatic church is deeply relational, rooted in a personal encounter with Jesus Christ. It is not merely about intellectual belief but about knowing God intimately, walking in communion with Him and experiencing His presence and power in everyday life.

In summary, faith in the charismatic church is a vibrant and dynamic force that fuels spiritual growth, empowers believers for supernatural living, and leads to a deeper intimacy with God. It is the catalyst for encountering the miraculous and experiencing the transformative power of God's kingdom here on earth.

The Controversies of the Charismatic Church

Like any religious movement, the charismatic church has faced its share of controversies.

While these controversies vary in nature and severity, they have often sparked debate, division, and reflection within the charismatic community.

Here are some notable controversies:

Prosperity Gospel:

One of the most widely debated controversies within the charismatic church is the Prosperity Gospel.

This teaching emphasizes that God rewards faith with financial prosperity and material blessings. Critics argue that it distorts biblical teachings on wealth and prosperity, exploits vulnerable individuals, and promotes a self-centered form of Christianity focused on personal gain rather than spiritual growth and sacrificial giving.

Financial Misconduct:

Some charismatic leaders have been embroiled in controversies related to financial misconduct, including allegations of misusing church funds, living lavish lifestyles at the expense of their followers, and engaging in unethical fundraising practices.

These scandals have damaged the reputation of the charismatic church and raised questions about accountability and stewardship within charismatic ministries.

Sexual Misconduct:

Instances of sexual misconduct and abuse involving charismatic leaders have also surfaced, leading to allegations of exploitation, manipulation, and betrayal of trust. These scandals have highlighted the need for greater transparency, accountability, and safeguarding measures within charismatic churches to protect vulnerable members from harm and abuse.

Theological Differences:

The charismatic movement encompasses a wide range of theological perspectives and doctrinal beliefs, leading to occasional disputes and controversies over theological issues such as the nature of spiritual gifts, the role of women in ministry, the interpretation of biblical prophecy, and the relationship between faith and works. These disagreements have sometimes resulted in division and fragmentation within the charismatic community.

Criticisms of Supernatural Manifestations:

Charismatic practices such as speaking in tongues, prophecy, and healing have been met with skepticism and criticism from both within and outside the church. Critics argue that some manifestations may be manipulated or exaggerated for dramatic effect, leading to questions about the authenticity and discernment of spiritual experiences within charismatic circles.

Ecumenical Relations:

The charismatic movement's emphasis on spiritual experiences and emotional worship has sometimes created tensions with more traditional or conservative branches of Christianity. Differences in worship styles, theological emphasis, and ecclesiastical structures have hindered ecumenical cooperation and dialogue, leading to division and mistrust between charismatic and non-charismatic Christians.

Cultural Appropriation:

Some critics have raised concerns about appropriating indigenous cultural practices and spiritual beliefs within charismatic worship and ministry. The adoption of certain cultural elements, such as music, dance, and religious symbols, without proper understanding or respect for their cultural significance has been seen as insensitive and disrespectful, leading to accusations of cultural imperialism and colonization.

Despite these controversies, many charismatic churches and leaders strive for authenticity, integrity, and accountability in their ministry, seeking to address and overcome challenges while remaining faithful to their core beliefs and mission.

The Charismatic Movement and TV Ministry

The connection between the charismatic church and TV broadcasting can be described as follows:

Television Ministry:

Many charismatic churches and ministries utilize television to broadcast their services, sermons, and evangelistic programs to a broader audience.

This medium allows charismatic leaders to reach viewers across geographical boundaries and connect with individuals who may not attend traditional church services in person.

Televangelism:

Televangelism, a form of religious broadcasting that features charismatic preachers delivering sermons and messages of faith, has been a significant aspect of the charismatic movement. Charismatic televangelists often emphasize healing, prosperity, and spiritual empowerment, attracting viewers seeking spiritual inspiration and guidance.

Global Reach:

Television broadcasting enables charismatic churches and ministries to reach an international audience, transcending cultural, linguistic, and geographical barriers.

Through satellite TV, cable networks, and online streaming platforms, millions worldwide can view charismatic programs, facilitating evangelistic outreach and discipleship on a massive scale.

Fundraising and Support:

Television broadcasts provide charismatic ministries a platform to solicit donations, support, and partnerships from viewers inspired by their message and ministry. Viewers are often encouraged to contribute financially to support the work of the ministry, fund humanitarian projects, and sustain the television broadcast itself.

Media Presence:

Television appearances by charismatic leaders and ministries also contribute to their media presence and public visibility. Interviews, talk shows, and documentary features allow charismatic figures to share their testimony, promote their books or products, and engage with mainstream audiences on spiritual and social issues.

Overall, television broadcasting plays a significant role in the outreach, growth, and influence of the charismatic church, serving as a powerful tool for spreading the message of faith, healing, and transformation to a diverse and global audience.

The Synergy Between TBN and the Charismatic Movement
Introduction:

Trinity Broadcasting Network (TBN) has played a significant role in shaping the landscape of Christian television and the Charismatic Movement over the past several decades. Founded by Paul and Jan Crouch in 1973, TBN has become one of the largest Christian television networks in the world, reaching millions of viewers with its programming that often reflects the beliefs and practices of the Charismatic Movement. This chapter explores the synergy between TBN and the Charismatic Movement, examining how the network has both influenced and been influenced by charismatic theology and spirituality.

The Rise of TBN:

TBN emerged when Christian television was still in its infancy. Still, the network quickly became a dominant force in the industry. With its emphasis on charismatic worship, preaching, and ministry, TBN appealed to a broad audience of believers hungry for spiritual content that reflected their own experiences and beliefs. The network's programming featured charismatic leaders such as Oral Roberts,

Kenneth Hagin, and Benny Hinn, who brought messages of healing, prosperity, and spiritual empowerment to viewers worldwide.

Charismatic Theology on TBN:

One of the hallmarks of TBN's programming has been its promotion of charismatic theology, which emphasizes the Holy Spirit's ongoing work in believers' lives. TBN has disseminated charismatic teachings on spiritual gifts, divine healing, and the power of prayer through televangelists, pastors, and teachers featured on the network.

Viewers have been encouraged to expect miracles, to pursue intimacy with God, and to experience the presence and power of the Holy Spirit in their own lives.

Platform for Charismatic Leaders:

TBN has provided a platform for charismatic leaders to reach a global audience with their message, enabling them to broadcast their services, conferences, and events to millions of viewers. This exposure has elevated the profile of charismatic leaders within the broader Christian community. It has helped to spread their influence beyond the walls of their own churches and ministries. Leaders such as Kenneth Copeland, Joyce Meyer, and Joel Osteen have become household names through their appearances on TBN, solidifying their status as influential voices within the Charismatic Movement.

Financial Support and Partnership:

TBN has also played a crucial role in providing financial support and partnerships to charismatic ministries and organizations.

Through its fundraising efforts and donor support, the network has helped to fund the work of charismatic churches, ministries, and missions around the world. Additionally, TBN has partnered with charismatic leaders and organizations to produce and distribute programming that promotes their shared theological and spiritual values.

Critiques and Controversies:

TBN has faced criticism and controversy despite its influence and popularity within the Charismatic Movement. Critics have raised concerns about the network's emphasis on prosperity theology, its promotion of televangelists with questionable ethics, and its perceived lack of accountability and transparency.

Additionally, TBN has been criticized for its commercialization of Christianity and its focus on entertainment and sensationalism at the expense of biblical truth and theological depth.

The Future of TBN and the Charismatic Movement:

As TBN continues to evolve and adapt to changing cultural and technological trends, its synergy with the Charismatic Movement will likely remain strong. The network will continue to serve as a platform for charismatic leaders to share their message and reach a global audience with their ministry. However, TBN also faces challenges in navigating the complexities of the modern media landscape and addressing the criticisms and controversies within the broader Christian community.

Ultimately, the future of TBN and the Charismatic Movement will depend on their ability to remain faithful to their core values and mission while adapting to the changing needs and preferences of their audience.

Conclusion:

The synergy between TBN and the Charismatic Movement has been a defining feature of both entities for decades. Through its programming, partnerships, and financial support, TBN has played a significant role in shaping the beliefs, practices, and influence of the Charismatic Movement worldwide.

While the network has faced criticism and controversy, its impact on the global Christian community cannot be denied. As TBN continues to evolve and adapt to new challenges and opportunities, its partnership with the Charismatic Movement will likely remain a central aspect of its identity and mission.

The Charismatic Movement and the 5 Fold Ministry

Within the charismatic church, the concept of the fivefold ministry refers to the biblical understanding of five distinct roles or functions of leadership and ministry described in Ephesians 4:11-13:

Apostles:

Apostles are seen as foundational leaders who are called to plant and establish churches, equip believers for ministry, and oversee the spiritual health and growth of the body of Christ. They often have a pioneering spirit, a vision for expansion and multiplication, and a strong emphasis on missions and evangelism.

Prophets:

Prophets are called to hear from God and communicate His messages to the church and the world. They often provide spiritual insight, guidance, and direction through words of prophecy, revelation, and interpretation of dreams and visions. Prophets also play a role in discerning spiritual dynamics, exposing deception, and calling the church to repentance and obedience.

Evangelists:

Evangelists are passionate communicators of the gospel who are called to proclaim the message of salvation and lead others to faith in Jesus Christ. They often have a gift for preaching, personal evangelism, and reaching out to unbelievers with compassion and conviction. Evangelists also play a role in equipping believers for evangelism and mobilizing the church for outreach and mission.

Pastors:

Pastors, also known as shepherds or overseers, are responsible for the care, nurture, and spiritual oversight of the flock of God. They provide pastoral care, counseling, and discipleship to believers, guiding them in their spiritual growth, maturity, and service within the church community. Pastors also have a role in teaching, preaching, and equipping believers for ministry.

Teachers:

Teachers are gifted in explaining and applying the truths of Scripture, helping believers understand and apply God's Word to their lives. They provide doctrinal instruction, theological training, and practical wisdom, equipping believers to discern truth from error, grow in their knowledge of God, and live out their faith with integrity and wisdom.

In the charismatic church, the fivefold ministry is often seen as essential for the health, growth, and maturity of the body of Christ. Believers are encouraged to recognize, affirm, and support individuals called to these leadership roles, recognizing that each ministry function is necessary for the church to fulfill its mission and purpose in the world. The goal of the fivefold ministry is to equip the saints for works of service, build up the body of Christ in unity and maturity, and advance the kingdom of God on earth.

The Charismatic Movement and the New Apostolic Reformation

The New Apostolic Reformation (NAR) is a movement within the charismatic Christian community that emerged in the late 20th century, advocating for restoring the ministry of apostles and prophets in the contemporary church. While the NAR is often associated with the charismatic church due to its emphasis on spiritual gifts, signs, and wonders, it is a distinct movement with its own theological distinctive and organizational structures.

Here's an overview of the New Apostolic Reformation and its relationship with the charismatic church:

Origins and Beliefs:

The NAR traces its roots to various streams of Pentecostal and charismatic Christianity and the broader charismatic renewal movement of the 20th century. It emerged in the 1990s as a response to perceived deficiencies in the church, particularly in spiritual authority, apostolic leadership, and societal transformation. The NAR emphasizes the restoration of the fivefold ministry described in Ephesians 4:11-13, focusing on apostles and prophets as foundational leaders for the church.

Apostolic Governance:

One of the fundamental tenets of the NAR is the belief in apostolic governance, which involves recognizing and submitting to apostolic authority within the church. Apostles are seen as spiritual fathers who provide oversight, direction, and alignment for the body of Christ, working in collaboration with other ministry gifts to advance God's kingdom on earth. This emphasis on apostolic leadership sets the NAR apart from traditional charismatic churches, which may have more decentralized or congregational forms of governance.

Prophetic Ministry:

The NAR strongly emphasizes the ministry of prophets and prophetic revelation, believing that God continues to speak to His people through prophetic words, dreams, and visions. Prophets are seen as spiritual seers who discern and declare God's will, direction, and purposes for individuals, churches, and nations. Prophetic ministry is valued for bringing alignment, correction, and encouragement to the body of Christ.

Spiritual Warfare and Dominion Theology:

Another distinctive feature of the NAR is its emphasis on spiritual warfare and the belief in the church's authority to exercise dominion and influence over the spiritual realm. This theology, often called Dominion Theology or Kingdom Now theology teaches that Christians are called to exert spiritual authority and reclaim territory from demonic influence, leading to societal transformation and the establishment of God's kingdom on earth.

Controversies and Criticisms:

The NAR has faced criticism and controversy from within and outside the charismatic community. Critics have raised concerns about the movement's hierarchical leadership structures, tendency towards authoritarianism, and its focus on supernatural signs and wonders. Some have also criticized certain teachings within the NAR, such as Dominion Theology, as being overly politicized or promoting a narrow interpretation of Christianity.

In summary, while the New Apostolic Reformation shares some commonalities with the charismatic church, including its emphasis on spiritual gifts, signs, and wonders, it is a distinct movement with its own theological emphases and organizational structures.

The NAR's advocacy for apostolic governance, prophetic ministry, and spiritual warfare sets it apart within the broader charismatic landscape, contributing to ongoing discussions and debates within the Christian community.

The core doctrines of the Charismatic Movement

The charismatic church encompasses a diverse range of theological perspectives and doctrinal beliefs. Still, several core doctrines are commonly emphasized within charismatic theology.

Here are some of the central doctrines of the charismatic church:

The Baptism of the Holy Spirit:

The charismatic church strongly emphasizes the baptism of the Holy Spirit as a distinct experience after salvation. Believers are encouraged to seek and receive the empowering presence of the Holy Spirit, often evidenced by speaking in tongues and the manifestation of spiritual gifts.

Spiritual Gifts:

Charismatic theology teaches that the Holy Spirit bestows spiritual gifts upon believers for the church's edification and the advancement of God's kingdom. As outlined in passages such as 1 Corinthians 12 and Romans 12, these gifts include prophecy, healing, miracles, tongues, interpretation of tongues, discernment, and others.

Divine Healing:

The charismatic church believes in the present-day ministry of divine healing, based on biblical promises such as those found in James 5:14-15 and Isaiah 53:5. Charismatic Christians pray for healing for physical, emotional, and spiritual ailments, trusting in God's power to bring about miraculous restoration and wholeness.

Prayer and Intercession:

Charismatic theology emphasizes the importance of prayer and intercession as essential spiritual disciplines for believers. Charismatic Christians are encouraged to cultivate a vibrant prayer life, seeking intimacy with God, spiritual breakthroughs, and manifesting His kingdom on earth through fervent, Spirit-led intercession.

Worship and Praise:

Charismatic worship is characterized by vibrant, expressive praise and worship that acknowledges the presence and majesty of God. Charismatic Christians believe in the power of worship to usher in God's presence, transform hearts, and release spiritual breakthroughs.

The Second Coming of Christ:

Charismatic theology affirms the biblical teaching of the second coming of Christ, emphasizing the imminent return of Jesus Christ to establish His kingdom on earth. Charismatic Christians anticipate the return of Christ with eager expectation and readiness, living in light of His promised return and the hope of eternal life.

The Charismatic Movement and the End Times

Introduction:

The Charismatic Movement has been characterized by its emphasis on spiritual gifts, signs, and wonders, leading many believers to speculate about its role in the end times. This chapter explores the intersection between the Charismatic Movement and eschatology, examining how charismatic theology and spirituality have influenced beliefs about the end times and the return of Christ.

From interpretations of biblical prophecy to expectations of supernatural manifestations, the Charismatic Movement has contributed to a diverse array of perspectives on the end times within the broader Christian community.

Interpretations of Biblical Prophecy:

One of the key ways in which the Charismatic Movement intersects with the end times is through interpretations of biblical prophecy. Charismatic theologians and preachers often approach prophetic texts with a sense of expectancy and openness to the supernatural, viewing them as a roadmap for understanding God's plan for the future. This perspective can lead to a heightened sense of anticipation regarding the fulfillment of end-time events and the return of Christ.

Some charismatic interpretations of biblical prophecy focus on spiritual warfare, revival, and the outpouring of the Holy Spirit in the last days. Believers are encouraged to pray for revival, engage in spiritual warfare against demonic forces, and expect supernatural manifestations of God's power as signs of the approaching end times.

This emphasis on the supernatural dimension of prophecy resonates with the experiential and charismatic spirituality of the movement.

Expectations of Supernatural Manifestations:

In addition to interpreting biblical prophecy, the Charismatic Movement often fosters expectations of supernatural manifestations in the end times. Charismatic believers are encouraged to anticipate signs and wonders, miracles, and spiritual encounters as evidence of God's presence and activity in the world. This expectation of the supernatural can fuel excitement and enthusiasm about the coming of the end times and the return of Christ.

Some charismatic leaders and ministries claim to have experienced supernatural phenomena such as angelic visitations, visions, and prophetic dreams that they interpret as signs of the end times.

These experiences are often shared with followers through books, sermons, and conferences, contributing to a culture of anticipation and readiness for the fulfillment of biblical prophecy.

The Role of Charismatic Leaders:

Charismatic leaders play a significant role in shaping beliefs about the end times within the movement. Through their preaching, teaching, and prophetic ministry, charismatic leaders often offer interpretations of biblical prophecy and insights into eschatological events that resonate with the experiences and expectations of their followers. Their authority and influence can shape the collective consciousness of the Charismatic Movement regarding the end times and the return of Christ.

Some charismatic leaders have gained notoriety for their bold predictions about the timing of end-time events, often drawing from biblical prophecy and contemporary world events to support their claims.

While these predictions can generate excitement and fervor among believers, they can also be met with skepticism and criticism if they fail to come to pass.

Discernment and Balance:

As believers navigate discussions about the end times within the Charismatic Movement, discernment and balance are essential. While the Charismatic Movement's emphasis on the supernatural and spiritual gifts can enrich our understanding of eschatology, it is crucial to approach interpretations of prophecy with humility and caution.

The diversity of perspectives within the Charismatic Movement reflects the complexity of biblical prophecy and the challenge of interpreting it in light of contemporary events.

Charismatic believers are called to cultivate a discerning spirit, testing all things against the standard of God's Word and seeking wisdom from trusted spiritual leaders and mentors. Rather than becoming consumed with speculation about the timing and details of end-time events, believers are encouraged to focus on living faithfully in the present, sharing the gospel, and fulfilling the Great Commission until the return of Christ.

Conclusion:

The Charismatic Movement's engagement with the end times reflects its vibrant spirituality, emphasis on the supernatural, and commitment to biblical prophecy.

While interpretations of prophecy and expectations of supernatural manifestations vary within the movement, the overarching theme of anticipation and readiness for the return of Christ permeates charismatic theology and spirituality.

As believers continue to wrestle with questions about the end times, may they be guided by discernment, humility, and a deep trust in God's sovereignty over the future.

End-Time Charismatic Writings: Exploring the Perspectives of Jonathan Cahn, Perry Stone, and John Hagee

Introduction:

In recent years, charismatic authors such as Jonathan Cahn, Perry Stone, and John Hagee have gained widespread recognition for their writings on end-time prophecy and biblical eschatology.

Through their books, articles, and teachings, these authors offer unique perspectives on the signs of the times, the return of Christ, and the role of believers in the last days. Let us examine the end-time charismatic writings of Jonathan Cahn, Perry Stone, and John Hagee, exploring their interpretations of biblical prophecy, their insights into current events, and the implications of their teachings for believers in the Charismatic Movement.

Jonathan Cahn: The Harbinger of End-Time Signs

Jonathan Cahn gained international acclaim with his bestselling book "The Harbinger," which explores the parallels between ancient Israel's disobedience and the United States' departure from God.

Cahn identifies a series of "harbingers," or prophetic signs, foreshadowing judgment and impending disaster. Drawing from biblical prophecy, Cahn warns of the consequences of national apostasy and calls believers to repentance and revival in the face of impending judgment.

His writings blend biblical prophecy with contemporary events, challenging readers to discern the signs of the times and prepare spiritually for the days ahead.

Perry Stone: Unveiling Mysteries of the End Times

Perry Stone is known for his in-depth studies of biblical prophecy and emphasis on decoding the mysteries of the end times.

Through his books, DVDs, and television programs, Stone explores a wide range of eschatological topics, including the prophetic significance of Israel, the rise of globalism, and the role of technology in fulfilling end-time prophecy. Stone's writings often draw from biblical prophecy and current events, offering insights into the spiritual significance of world events and encouraging believers to remain vigilant and prayerful in anticipation of Christ's return.

His teachings emphasize the importance of discerning the times and living with a sense of urgency in light of the signs of the times.

John Hagee: Advocating for Israel and Prophecy

John Hagee is a prominent voice within the Charismatic Movement, known for his advocacy for Israel and his teachings on biblical prophecy.

Through his books and ministry, Hagee emphasizes the prophetic significance of Israel's restoration and the role of the Jewish people in God's end-time plans. He interprets current events through the lens of biblical prophecy, pointing to the alignment of nations and the rise of geopolitical tensions as signs of the approaching end times. Hagee's writings often emphasize the importance of standing with Israel and understanding the prophetic significance of events unfolding in the Middle East.

He encourages believers to pray for the peace of Jerusalem and to remain vigilant in light of the signs of the times.

Themes and Commonalities:

While each author brings a unique perspective to the study of end-time prophecy, some common themes and motifs run throughout their writings.

All three authors emphasize the importance of discerning the signs of the times and understanding the prophetic significance of current events. They encourage believers to live with a sense of urgency and expectancy in light of Christ's imminent return.

Additionally, they emphasize the need for spiritual preparedness, repentance, and revival in the face of impending judgment.

Conclusion:

The end-time charismatic writings of Jonathan Cahn, Perry Stone, and John Hagee offer valuable insights into the signs of the times and the prophetic significance of current events. Through their teachings, believers are challenged to discern the times, remain vigilant, and prepare spiritually for the days ahead.

While each author brings a unique perspective to the study of end-time prophecy, their collective emphasis on spiritual discernment, repentance, and revival serves as a timely reminder of the urgency of the hour and the importance of being spiritually prepared for Christ's return.

As believers engage with their writings, may they be inspired to live with faith, hope, and expectancy in anticipation of the fulfillment of God's end-time purposes.

Spiritual Warfare:

Charismatic theology recognizes the reality of spiritual warfare and the believer's role in battles against demonic forces and spiritual strongholds. Charismatic Christians are equipped with spiritual weapons such as prayer, fasting, and the Word of God to overcome the powers of darkness and advance God's kingdom agenda.

These core doctrines, along with others, such as salvation by grace through faith, the authority of Scripture, and the priesthood of all believers, form the foundation of charismatic theology and practice, shaping the beliefs and experiences of charismatic Christians worldwide.

"Hypergrace," "hyperprosperity," and "hyperfaith" are terms often used to describe certain theological teachings and movements within the charismatic and broader evangelical Christian community.

While these terms may have different interpretations and connotations depending on one's perspective, they generally refer to an exaggerated or imbalanced emphasis on grace, prosperity, and faith, respectively.

Here's an overview of each concept:

Hypergrace:

Definition:

Hypergrace is a term used to describe an extreme or imbalanced emphasis on the grace of God in Christian theology. It suggests an overemphasis on the concept of grace to the exclusion of other critical biblical teachings, such as repentance, obedience, and holiness.

Characteristics:

Hypergrace teachings often downplay the importance of moral behavior and righteous living, sometimes leading to antinomianism (the belief that Christians are not bound by moral law). Critics argue that hypergrace can lead to a cheapening of God's grace and disregarding the need for repentance and transformation in the Christian life.

Criticism:

Critics of hypergrace theology raise concerns about its potential to undermine the seriousness of sin, diminish the call to holy living, and distort the gospel's message by emphasizing grace at the expense of other biblical truths.

Hyperprosperity:

Definition:

Hyperprosperity, also known as the prosperity gospel or health and wealth gospel, is a theological perspective that emphasizes material blessings, financial prosperity, and physical well-being as signs of God's favor and blessings.

Characteristics:

Hyperprosperity teachings often promise financial abundance, success, and good health to believers who have enough faith and sow financial seeds (i.e., give money to the church or ministry). Adherents of hyperprosperity theology may claim that poverty and sickness are signs of spiritual deficiency or lack of faith.

Criticism:

Critics of hyperprosperity theology argue that it distorts the gospel's message by equating God's blessings primarily with material wealth and success. They also point out that it can lead to exploitation, manipulation, and guilt-tripping of believers who are encouraged to give sacrificially in hopes of receiving material blessings in return.

Hyperfaith:

Definition:

Hyperfaith, also known as "name it and claim it" or "word of faith" theology, is a belief system that emphasizes the power of faith-filled words to create reality and bring about desired outcomes in every area of life.

Characteristics:

Hyperfaith teachings emphasize the importance of positive confession, visualization, and the speaking of faith-filled declarations to claim God's promises and overcome obstacles. Adherents may believe that speaking words of faith can "activate" God's power and bring about supernatural results.

Criticism:

Critics of hyperfaith theology argue that it can lead to a simplistic and formulaic approach to faith, overlooking life's complexities and God's sovereignty. They caution against the idea that faith guarantees material success or immunity from suffering, pointing out that biblical faith involves trust in God's character and sovereignty, regardless of outward circumstances.

While these concepts have gained popularity in some segments of the charismatic and evangelical Christian community, they are also subject to criticism and debate within broader theological circles. As with any theological perspective, it is essential to critically examine teachings in light of Scripture and to seek a balanced understanding of biblical truth.

Charismatic Chaos?

"Charismatic Chaos" is a book by John F. MacArthur Jr., an influential pastor, author, and theologian within the Reformed tradition. Published in 1992, the book critically analyzes the charismatic movement, raising concerns about what MacArthur perceives as theological errors, doctrinal deviations, and spiritual dangers within the movement.

While "Charismatic Chaos" primarily represents a negative assessment of the charismatic movement, it has undoubtedly influenced the discourse within the broader evangelical community, including the charismatic church.

Here's how "Charismatic Chaos" has influenced the charismatic church:

Exposure of Controversial Practices:

"Charismatic Chaos" highlighted certain controversial practices and teachings within the charismatic movement that were perceived as aberrant or unorthodox. MacArthur highlighted phenomena such as "holy laughter," "slain in the Spirit," and exaggerated claims of miraculous healings, raising questions about their biblical basis and theological legitimacy.

Critique of Prosperity Theology:

One of the key criticisms in "Charismatic Chaos" is directed towards the prosperity gospel, a theological perspective that emphasizes material wealth and financial prosperity as signs of God's favor and blessings. MacArthur argues against the prosperity gospel's emphasis on financial giving, positive confession, and faith for material gain, cautioning against its potential to mislead and exploit believers.

Emphasis on Biblical Discernment:

"Charismatic Chaos" underscores the importance of biblical discernment and theological clarity within the charismatic movement. MacArthur encourages believers to test all spiritual experiences, teachings, and manifestations against the standard of Scripture, urging them to reject anything that deviates from biblical truth.

Impact on Evangelical Thought:

While "Charismatic Chaos" has been controversial within the charismatic movement, it has also influenced evangelical thought and discourse on charismatic theology and practice.

The book has prompted discussions and debates within the broader evangelical community about the nature of spiritual gifts, the validity of certain charismatic practices, and the need for theological discernment in evaluating charismatic claims.

Strengthening of Reformed and Cessationist Perspectives:

"Charismatic Chaos" has reinforced the perspectives of Reformed and cessationist theologians who advocate for a cessation of certain charismatic gifts, such as tongues and prophecy, after the apostolic age. MacArthur's book has provided theological arguments and biblical evidence supporting cessationism, contributing to its continued advocacy within specific segments of the evangelical community.

While "Charismatic Chaos" has been criticized by proponents of the charismatic movement for its negative portrayal and selective analysis, it has nevertheless played a significant role in shaping the conversation about charismatic theology and practice within broader evangelical circles.

Its influence has prompted believers to critically evaluate charismatic claims, seek biblical grounding for spiritual experiences, and pursue theological discernment in navigating the complexities of the charismatic movement.

The "American Gospel"

"American Gospel" is a documentary film series that explores and critiques various aspects of the prosperity gospel, word of faith movement, and other theological perspectives within evangelical Christianity.

Directed by Brandon Kimber, the series consists of two installments: "American Gospel: Christ Alone" (2018) and "American Gospel: Christ Crucified" (2019). While "American Gospel" primarily focuses on the broader evangelical landscape, it also sheds light on certain teachings and practices within the charismatic church, particularly those associated with the prosperity gospel and hyper-faith movements.

Here's how "American Gospel" exposed the charismatic church:
Critique of Prosperity Theology:

One of the central themes of "American Gospel" is its critique of the prosperity gospel. This theological perspective emphasizes material wealth and financial prosperity as signs of God's favor and blessings. The documentary exposes the unbiblical nature of prosperity theology and its harmful effects on believers, highlighting testimonies of individuals who have been misled, exploited, or disillusioned by prosperity preachers within the charismatic movement.

Examination of Word of Faith Teachings:

"American Gospel" also examines the Word Of Faith movement, emphasizing the power of positive confession and faith-filled words to create reality and bring about desired outcomes.

The documentary critiques certain teachings within the Word of Faith movement, such as the "name it and claim it" doctrine and the idea that faith guarantees health, wealth, and success.

It exposes the dangers of hyper-faith theology and its potential to lead believers into disillusionment and spiritual manipulation.

Comparison with Biblical Christianity:

"American Gospel" presents biblical Christianity as distinct from and opposed to the teachings of the prosperity gospel and word of faith movement.

The documentary contrasts the true message of the gospel, centered on the person and work of Jesus Christ, with the false promises and distortions propagated by prosperity preachers.

It emphasizes the importance of understanding and proclaiming the true gospel message of salvation by grace through faith in Christ alone.

Testimonies and Expert Analysis:

"American Gospel" features testimonies from individuals impacted by prosperity theology and Word of Faith teachings and insights from theologians, pastors, and scholars who offer critical analysis and biblical perspectives on these movements.

The documentary provides a comprehensive examination of the theological, historical, and cultural factors that contributed to the rise of prosperity theology within the charismatic and evangelical churches.

Call to Discernment and Gospel Clarity:

Ultimately, the "American Gospel" calls for discernment and gospel clarity within the charismatic church and broader evangelical community.

It challenges believers to examine their beliefs and practices in light of Scripture, reject false teachings that distort the gospel's true message, and embrace the centrality of Christ and His finished work on the cross as the foundation of their faith.

While "American Gospel" may be controversial within certain charismatic circles, it has sparked essential conversations and reflections about the relationship between prosperity theology, Word of Faith teachings, and biblical Christianity. The documentary has exposed the dangers of theological error and spiritual manipulation within the charismatic church while pointing believers towards a deeper understanding of the true gospel message of salvation and grace.

Strange Fire?

"Strange Fire" is a book by John F. MacArthur Jr., a prominent pastor, author, and theologian within the Reformed tradition, and the accompanying Strange Fire Conference held in 2013. The book and conference were highly critical of certain practices and teachings within the charismatic movement, particularly those related to exercising spiritual gifts such as prophecy, tongues, and healing.

Here's how "Strange Fire" has impacted the discourse within the charismatic church:

Critique of Charismatic Practices:

"Strange Fire" presents a comprehensive critique of what MacArthur perceives as unbiblical and harmful practices within the charismatic movement.

MacArthur argues against specific charismatic manifestations, such as speaking in tongues, prophetic utterances, and claims of miraculous healings, which he views as counterfeit or fraudulent. He raises concerns about the lack of biblical grounding, discernment, and accountability in charismatic circles, cautioning against the potential for deception and spiritual manipulation.

Rejection of Charismatic Theology:

In addition to critiquing charismatic practices, "Strange Fire" also challenges the theological foundations of the charismatic movement, including its emphasis on the continuation of miraculous gifts such as prophecy and tongues. MacArthur advocates for a cessationist perspective, which teaches that certain miraculous gifts ceased with the apostolic age and are no longer operative in the church today. He argues that the charismatic movement promotes a distorted understanding of the Holy Spirit and undermines the sufficiency of Scripture.

Controversy and Debate:

The publication of "Strange Fire" and the accompanying conference sparked controversy and debate within the evangelical community, including among charismatic Christians.

While some charismatic leaders and believers rejected MacArthur's criticisms as unfounded and divisive, others acknowledged the need for greater theological discernment and accountability within the charismatic movement.

The book prompted reflections and discussions about the nature of spiritual gifts, the role of experience versus Scripture, and the importance of biblical discernment in evaluating charismatic claims.

Impact on Charismatic Theology:

While "Strange Fire" was met with resistance and criticism from proponents of the charismatic movement, it nevertheless influenced the discourse and theology within certain segments of the charismatic church.

The book prompted believers to critically examine charismatic practices and teachings in light of Scripture, leading some to reconsider their views on issues such as the cessation of certain spiritual gifts and the need for more significant theological grounding and accountability.

Call for Reformation:

Ultimately, "Strange Fire" served as a call for reformation and renewal within the charismatic church, urging believers to return to a biblical understanding of the Holy Spirit and spiritual gifts.

While MacArthur's criticisms were met with controversy and disagreement, they also prompted essential conversations about the proper exercise of spiritual gifts, the dangers of excess and abuse, and the importance of upholding the authority of Scripture in all matters of faith and practice.

In summary, "Strange Fire" contributed to a broader conversation within the charismatic church and evangelical community about spiritual gifts' nature, purpose, and exercise.

While it was met with criticism and disagreement, it also prompted reflections and introspection among believers, leading to a renewed emphasis on biblical discernment, theological clarity, and spiritual integrity within the charismatic movement.

An In-Depth Analysis of "God, Greed, and the (Prosperity) Gospel" by Costi Hinn

Abstract:

This Chapter provides an in-depth analysis of Costi Hinn's book, "God, Greed, and the (Prosperity) Gospel," exploring its themes, arguments, and significance in contemporary Christian theology and practice.

It also examines Costi Hinn's personal testimonies. It reflects on the broader implications of his work for discussing prosperity theology.

Additionally, it compares and contrasts Hinn's book with other works on the same subject matter, providing insights into the diverse perspectives within the broader conversation surrounding prosperity gospel theology.

Introduction:

Costi Hinn, a former insider of prosperity gospel preaching, offers a compelling critique of the movement in his book, "God, Greed, and the (Prosperity) Gospel."

Drawing from his personal experiences and theological insights, Hinn challenges the teachings and practices of prosperity theology while offering a vision for a more authentic and biblically grounded expression of Christian faith.

This Chapter explores the key themes and arguments presented in Hinn's book, examines his personal testimonies, and evaluates the broader implications of his work for the study of prosperity gospel theology.

Summary of "God, Greed, and the (Prosperity) Gospel":

In "God, Greed, and the (Prosperity) Gospel," Costi Hinn critically examines the prosperity gospel movement, exposing its flaws, contradictions, and harmful consequences.

Drawing from his experiences growing up as the nephew of prominent prosperity preacher Benny Hinn, Costi offers firsthand insights into the inner workings of the movement and the motivations behind its teachings.

One of the book's central themes is the pervasiveness of greed within the prosperity gospel, as preachers promise material wealth and financial blessings in exchange for faith and financial giving.

Costi argues that this emphasis on material prosperity distorts the true message of the gospel, leading believers away from the teachings of Jesus and into a pursuit of wealth and success.

Costi also highlights the manipulative tactics used by prosperity preachers to extract money from their followers, including emotional manipulation, false promises, and coercive fundraising techniques.

He shares personal anecdotes and testimonies of individuals who have been exploited and deceived by prosperity preachers, illustrating the damaging impact of the movement on vulnerable believers.

Throughout the book, Costi emphasizes the importance of biblical discernment and spiritual maturity in evaluating the claims of prosperity theology.

He encourages believers to study the Scriptures carefully, test all teachings against the standard of God's Word, and seek a deeper relationship with Jesus Christ apart from the allure of material wealth.

Personal Testimonies of Costi Hinn:

As the nephew of Benny Hinn, one of the most prominent prosperity preachers in the world, Costi Hinn offers a unique perspective on the inner workings of the prosperity gospel movement.

In "God, Greed, and the (Prosperity) Gospel," Costi shares personal testimonies of his experiences growing up in the Hinn family and immersed in the world of prosperity preaching.

Costi recounts how he was initially drawn to the glamour and excitement of his uncle's ministry, believing that prosperity theology offered the key to success and happiness.

However, as he grew older and began to question the movement's teachings, Costi experienced a crisis of faith that ultimately led him to renounce prosperity theology and embrace a more biblically grounded understanding of Christianity.

One of the most powerful testimonies in the book is Costi's account of his journey out of the prosperity gospel and into a deeper relationship with Jesus Christ. He describes wrestling with difficult questions, confronting the inconsistencies of prosperity theology, and ultimately finding freedom and joy in a faith centered on Christ alone.

Costi's personal testimonies serve as a compelling backdrop to his critique of prosperity theology, providing readers with insight into the human side of the movement and the toll it can take on individuals and families. His willingness to share his own struggles and doubts adds credibility to his arguments and underscores the urgency of his message.

Comparison with Other Works on Prosperity Gospel Theology:

Costi Hinn's "God, Greed, and the (Prosperity) Gospel" is part of a broader conversation within Christian theology about the nature and impact of prosperity gospel teachings.

While Hinn's book offers a personal and insider perspective on the movement, it also builds on the work of other scholars and theologians who have critiqued prosperity theology from various perspectives.

One notable comparison is with Joel Osteen's "Your Best Life Now," a bestselling book that promotes a message of prosperity and success based on biblical principles. While Osteen's book emphasizes the power of positive thinking and personal empowerment, Hinn's book challenges the underlying assumptions of prosperity theology and exposes its dangers.

Similarly, Kenneth Copeland's "The Laws of Prosperity" presents a systematic theology of prosperity based on biblical principles and promises. Hinn's book offers a counter-narrative to Copeland's teachings, arguing that prosperity theology distorts the true message of the gospel and leads believers astray from the path of discipleship and self-sacrifice.

In contrast to these works, "God, Greed, and the (Prosperity) Gospel" offers a more critical and nuanced perspective on prosperity theology, drawing on personal testimonies, theological insights, and biblical analysis to make its case against the movement.

Costi Hinn contributes to a deeper understanding of the theological, ethical, and practical issues at stake by situating his book within the broader context of the prosperity gospel debate.

Conclusion:

In conclusion, Costi Hinn's "God, Greed, and the (Prosperity) Gospel" offers a compelling critique of prosperity theology, drawing from personal testimonies, theological insights, and biblical analysis to expose the dangers of the movement.

Through his book, Hinn challenges believers to question the teachings of prosperity preachers, discern the true message of the gospel, and pursue a deeper relationship with Jesus Christ apart from the lure of material wealth.

By sharing his journey out of the prosperity gospel, Costi Hinn offers hope and encouragement to those struggling with doubts or questions about their faith.

As a thoughtful and insightful exploration of one of the most controversial movements in contemporary Christianity, "God, Greed, and the (Prosperity) Gospel" contributes to the ongoing conversation about the nature and impact of prosperity theology.

The Mega-Church debate

Charismatic and mega-churches are distinct but sometimes overlapping phenomena within contemporary Christianity.

While not all mega-churches are charismatic, and not all charismatic churches are mega-churches, there are significant connections and similarities between the two.

Here's how they intersect:

Growth and Influence:

The charismatic movement and the mega-church phenomenon have experienced significant growth and influence within global Christianity. Charismatic churches emphasize the supernatural work of the Holy Spirit, spiritual gifts, and dynamic worship experiences, which often attract large numbers of believers seeking spiritual encounters and empowerment.

On the other hand, Mega churches are characterized by their large congregations, expansive facilities, and diverse ministries, catering to the needs of thousands of attendees through innovative programming and outreach efforts.

Contemporary Worship:

Charismatic and mega-churches prioritize contemporary worship styles featuring vibrant music, expressive praise, and multimedia presentations.

Charismatic worship often includes spontaneous prayer, prophetic singing, and the manifestation of spiritual gifts, creating an atmosphere of spiritual fervor and engagement. Mega churches utilize modern technology and production values to enhance the worship experience, with professional bands, theatrical lighting, and high-quality sound systems contributing to an immersive worship environment.

Emphasis on Leadership:

Charismatic churches and mega-churches often have strong, charismatic leaders at the helm who play a central role in shaping the church's vision, culture, and direction.

These leaders may have dynamic preaching styles, personal charisma, and a vision for growth and expansion. In charismatic churches, leaders are often viewed as spiritual authorities who exercise spiritual gifts such as prophecy, healing, and discernment.

In mega-churches, leaders may also function as visionary CEOs, overseeing large staff teams and multi-million-dollar budgets to manage the complex operations of the church.

Community and Connection:

Despite their large size, both charismatic and mega-churches strongly emphasize fostering community and connection among their members.

Small groups, home fellowships, and ministry teams allow believers to build relationships, receive pastoral care, and engage in discipleship and ministry.

Charismatic churches may also emphasize the importance of spiritual accountability, mentorship, and impartation from leaders to members, fostering a sense of family and belonging within the congregation.

Outreach and Impact:

Charismatic and mega-churches often emphasize outreach and social impact locally and globally. They may engage in various forms of community service, humanitarian aid, and mission outreach, demonstrating the love and compassion of Christ to those in need.

With their large congregations and resources, Mega-churches are particularly well-positioned to spearhead initiatives such as disaster relief, poverty alleviation, and evangelistic campaigns that make a tangible difference in the lives of individuals and communities.

In summary, while there are distinct differences between charismatic and mega-churches, they share common traits such as a focus on contemporary worship, strong leadership, emphasis on community, and commitment to outreach and impact.

Together, they represent vibrant expressions of modern Christianity, attracting believers from diverse backgrounds and contributing to the global expansion of the Christian faith.

The Charismatic Movement and the Church Growth Movement

The charismatic church and the Church Growth Movement (CGM) are two significant phenomena within contemporary Christianity that have intersected and influenced each other in various ways.

While they are distinct movements with different emphases and origins, they share common goals of expanding the influence and impact of the church. Here's how they relate to each other:

Emphasis on Growth:

Both the charismatic church and the Church Growth Movement share a strong emphasis on numerical growth and expansion.

Charismatic churches often experience rapid growth through evangelistic outreach, dynamic worship services, and the demonstration of spiritual gifts, attracting new believers seeking spiritual encounters and empowerment.

Similarly, the Church Growth Movement, spearheaded by leaders such as Donald McGavran and C. Peter Wagner, advocates for strategic methods and principles to facilitate the growth of churches, emphasizing factors such as homogeneity, evangelism, and leadership development.

Innovative Outreach Strategies:

Charismatic churches and the Church Growth Movement are known for their innovative approaches to outreach and evangelism. Charismatic churches utilize dynamic worship services, small groups, and personal testimonies to engage seekers and draw them into the church's life.

The Church Growth Movement, meanwhile, promotes research-based strategies and principles for reaching specific demographic groups, adapting ministry approaches to cultural contexts, and maximizing the effectiveness of evangelistic efforts.

Leadership Development:

Both movements prioritize leadership development as key to church growth and effectiveness. Charismatic churches often identify and cultivate leaders from within their congregations, equipping them for ministry through training programs, mentorship, and hands-on experience.

Similarly, the Church Growth Movement emphasizes the importance of effective leadership in fostering healthy, growing churches, advocating for intentional strategies for identifying, training, and empowering leaders to fulfill their potential and impact.

Utilization of Technology and Media:

Charismatic churches and the Church Growth Movement leverage technology and media to enhance their outreach and communication efforts. Charismatic churches often utilize multimedia presentations, live streaming services, and social media platforms to reach a wider audience and engage believers beyond the confines of the physical church building.

The Church Growth Movement promotes marketing techniques, communication tools, and media resources to effectively convey the gospel's message and attract seekers to the church.

Cultural Adaptation:

Both movements recognize the importance of cultural adaptation and contextualization in reaching diverse communities with the gospel message. Charismatic churches embrace cultural diversity and often incorporate elements of ethnic music, dance, and expression into their worship services, creating a welcoming environment for people from different cultural backgrounds.

The Church Growth Movement advocates for sensitivity to cultural norms and preferences in ministry contexts. It encourages churches to adapt their methods and approaches to effectively connect with and engage diverse audiences.

In summary, while the charismatic church and the Church Growth Movement are distinct movements with different emphases and methodologies, they share common goals of expanding the influence and impact of the church through innovative outreach, leadership development, and cultural adaptation.

Together, they represent dynamic expressions of contemporary Christianity, contributing to the global growth and vitality of the church.

The 7 Mountains Mandate

The "7 Mountains" theory, also known as the "7 Mountains Mandate" or "7 Mountains of Influence," is a worldview and strategic framework that has gained traction within specific segments of the charismatic and evangelical Christian community.

The theory proposes seven key spheres or "mountains" of societal influence. Christians are called to occupy and influence these spheres with biblical values and principles. Here's how the charismatic church relates to the 7 Mountains theory:

Identifying the Spheres:

The 7 Mountains theory identifies seven spheres of influence in society that are believed to shape culture and society.

These spheres include:

- Government
- Education
- Media
- Business
- Arts & Entertainment
- Family
- Religion

Mission and Influence:

The 7 Mountains theory is often embraced within the charismatic church as a strategic framework for cultural engagement and societal transformation. Charismatic Christians view themselves as agents of change called to infiltrate and influence these spheres with the values and principles of the kingdom of God.

They believe that occupying leadership positions and influence in these spheres can impact society for Christ and bring about positive change.

Dominion Theology:

The 7 Mountains theory is sometimes associated with Dominion Theology, which teaches that Christians are called to exercise dominion and authority over the earth as stewards and representatives of God.

Charismatic Christians who embrace the 7 Mountains theory often emphasize the idea of reclaiming territory from secular or ungodly influence and establishing God's kingdom on earth.

Strategic Engagement:

Charismatic churches and ministries that subscribe to the 7 Mountains theory often engage in strategic initiatives to influence the spheres of society identified in the theory.

This may include training believers for leadership roles in government, education, media, business, and other sectors and organizing prayer initiatives, advocacy campaigns, and outreach efforts to impact culture and policy.

Cultural Relevance:

The 7 Mountains theory resonates with the charismatic emphasis on cultural relevance and engagement. Charismatic churches often seek to engage with contemporary culture and address issues relevant to society, viewing the spheres of influence identified in theory as strategic areas for ministry and mission.

Criticism and Debate:

While the 7 Mountains theory has gained popularity within specific segments of the charismatic church, it is not without its critics.

Some theologians and scholars raise concerns about the potential for overemphasis on cultural transformation at the expense of the gospel's proclamation and the church's spiritual mission.

Others caution against a narrow interpretation of the theory that may prioritize political power or cultural influence over the values of the kingdom of God.

In summary, the 7 Mountains theory represents a strategic framework for cultural engagement and societal transformation that has gained traction within specific segments of the charismatic church.

While it is embraced by some as a means of advancing the kingdom of God in society, it is also subject to debate and criticism within the broader Christian community. Ultimately, its impact on the charismatic church depends on how it is interpreted, applied, and integrated into the wider mission and vision of the church.

The transition from Pentecostalism to Charismatic

The transition from Pentecostalism to the charismatic movement represents a significant shift within the broader charismatic and evangelical Christian landscape.

While Pentecostalism and the charismatic movement share common roots and theological emphases, there are distinct differences in their historical development, theological perspectives, and organizational structures.

Here's an overview of the transition from Pentecostalism to the charismatic movement:

Origins of Pentecostalism:

Pentecostalism emerged in the late 19th and early 20th centuries as a distinct movement within Protestant Christianity, with roots in the Holiness and Wesleyan traditions.

The modern Pentecostal movement is often traced back to the Azusa Street Revival in Los Angeles, California, led by William J. Seymour in 1906. Pentecostalism emphasizes the baptism of the Holy Spirit, speaking in tongues, and the manifestation of spiritual gifts as essential aspects of the Christian experience.

Spread of Pentecostalism:

Pentecostalism experienced rapid growth and expansion in the early 20th century, spreading throughout North America and across the globe through missionary efforts and evangelistic campaigns. Pentecostal denominations such as the Assemblies of God, Church of God in Christ, and Pentecostal Holiness Church were established, providing organizational structures and theological frameworks for Pentecostal believers.

Charismatic Renewal:

In the 1960s and 1970s, a new wave of spiritual renewal and revival emerged within mainline Protestant and Catholic churches, known as the charismatic renewal or charismatic movement.

This movement was characterized by a renewed emphasis on the Holy Spirit, spiritual gifts, and experiences of empowerment and encounter with God.

Many individuals within these churches began to experience manifestations such as speaking in tongues, prophetic utterances, and healing, similar to those in Pentecostalism.

Transition and Integration:

As the charismatic movement gained momentum, many Pentecostal believers and churches were drawn to the new expressions of spirituality and worship emerging within the charismatic renewal.

Some Pentecostal denominations, such as the Assemblies of God, embraced the charismatic movement and welcomed charismatic experiences and practices within their congregations.

Other Pentecostal churches experienced a more gradual transition, integrating charismatic elements into their worship services and ministry practices while maintaining their Pentecostal identity.

Diversity and Continuity:

The transition from Pentecostalism to the charismatic movement was characterized by diversity and continuity. While some Pentecostal churches and denominations fully embraced the charismatic movement and its emphasis on ecumenical unity and spiritual renewal; others maintained a distinct Pentecostal identity and theological perspective.

Nevertheless, the charismatic movement brought together believers from diverse theological backgrounds, denominations, and traditions, fostering a spirit of unity and collaboration centered on the person and work of the Holy Spirit.

In summary, the transition from Pentecostalism to the charismatic movement represents a significant development within contemporary

Christianity, characterized by a renewal of spiritual vitality, a rediscovery of spiritual gifts, and a spirit of ecumenical unity among believers from diverse traditions.

While Pentecostalism and the charismatic movement have distinct historical origins and theological emphases, they share common roots in the belief in the power and presence of the Holy Spirit and the expectation of spiritual encounters and empowerment in the believer's life.

Telethons

Telethons, a form of televised fundraising event, have been utilized by various religious and secular organizations to raise funds, promote causes, and engage with audiences.

While telethons are not exclusive to the charismatic church, they have been employed by some charismatic ministries to support their ministries, reach broader audiences, and generate financial resources.

Here's how the charismatic church relates to telethons:

Fundraising and Financial Support:

Charismatic churches and ministries often rely on donations and financial support from their congregants and supporters to fund their activities, programs, and outreach efforts.

Telethons allow charismatic ministries to appeal to viewers for financial contributions through pledges, donations, or partnerships.

These funds may support various initiatives, such as mission trips, humanitarian aid projects, media outreach, and facility maintenance.

Television and Media Outreach:

Many charismatic ministries have utilized television and media platforms to reach wider audiences with their message and ministry.

Telethons allow charismatic churches and ministries to broadcast their programs, testimonies, and messages to viewers across different regions and demographics, potentially reaching individuals who may not otherwise attend traditional church services or events.

Telethons often feature dynamic worship, inspirational messages, and personal testimonies to engage viewers and elicit a response.

Spiritual and Emotional Appeal:

Charismatic telethons often incorporate spiritual and emotional appeal elements to encourage viewers to participate and support the ministry's work.

This may include testimonies of changed lives, reports of miracles or healings, and messages of hope and encouragement.

Charismatic leaders and speakers may also invite viewers to experience personal transformation through faith, prayer, and financial partnership with the ministry.

Controversies and Criticisms:

While telethons can be effective fundraising and outreach tools, they have also been criticized and debated within the charismatic church.

Critics raise concerns about the manipulation of emotions, the emphasis on financial prosperity, and the potential misuse of funds within some charismatic telethons.

There have been instances of charismatic televangelists facing scrutiny over allegations of financial impropriety, extravagant lifestyles, and false promises of miraculous blessings in exchange for donations.

Transparency and Accountability:

In response to criticism and concerns about transparency and accountability, some charismatic ministries have improved their financial practices and governance structures.

This may include financial transparency, accountability mechanisms, and oversight processes to ensure that donations are used responsibly and following the ministry's stated mission and values.

In summary, while telethons have been utilized by some charismatic churches and ministries as a means of fundraising and outreach, they have also been subject to criticism and controversy.

Charismatic telethons can be practical tools for engaging with audiences, promoting causes, and generating financial support.

Still, they also require careful stewardship, integrity, and accountability to maintain trust and credibility within the broader Christian community.

Splintering and diversity

The charismatic church has been a catalyst for forming various sects and splinter groups within Christianity, each with distinct beliefs, practices, and organizational structures.

While the charismatic movement is diverse and encompasses a wide range of theological perspectives and expressions, certain factions and individuals have sought to establish independent ministries, denominations, or fellowships.

Here's how the charismatic church has contributed to the formation of sects and splinter groups:

Theological Diversity:

The charismatic movement is characterized by its theological diversity, encompassing a broad spectrum of beliefs and practices related to spiritual gifts, divine healing, prophecy, and other supernatural manifestations.

Within this diverse landscape, individuals and groups may gravitate towards particular theological emphases or interpretations, forming sects or splinter groups that align with their specific convictions.

Leadership Dynamics:

Charismatic churches and ministries often strongly emphasize the role of charismatic leaders and figures who wield significant influence and authority within their spheres of influence.

In some cases, disagreements or conflicts over leadership dynamics, doctrinal interpretation, or ministry direction may lead to schisms or divisions within charismatic communities, forming new sects or splinter groups.

Doctrinal Differences:

Despite sharing common theological roots, charismatic groups and individuals may hold divergent views on critical doctrinal issues, such as the nature of spiritual gifts, the authority of Scripture, the role of women in ministry, and eschatology (the study of end times).

These doctrinal differences can sometimes become points of contention or division within charismatic communities, leading to sects or factions that align with specific doctrinal positions.

Personalities and Egos:

Charismatic leaders and personalities play a significant role in shaping the identity and direction of charismatic churches and ministries.

In some cases, personal ambition, ego, or charismatic leadership styles may contribute to conflicts or power struggles within charismatic communities, splintering off dissatisfied members or factions seeking to establish their own independent ministries or fellowships.

Theological Innovation:

The charismatic movement is known for its openness to theological innovation and experimentation, as believers seek to discern and apply biblical principles in light of contemporary cultural and spiritual contexts.

While this openness can foster creativity and dynamism within the movement, it can also give rise to theological outliers or fringe groups that espouse unconventional or heterodox beliefs, leading to sects or splinter groups that diverge from mainstream charismatic orthodoxy.

In summary, while the charismatic church has been a source of spiritual renewal, vitality, and innovation within Christianity, it has also been marked by theological diversity, leadership dynamics, doctrinal differences, and personality-driven dynamics that have contributed to forming sects and splinter groups.

While some of these groups may represent legitimate expressions of charismatic Christianity, others may exhibit characteristics of cultic behavior, manipulation, or doctrinal deviation, highlighting the need for discernment and accountability within the broader charismatic community.

Positive Confession

Positive confession is a theological concept commonly associated with the charismatic movement, particularly within the prosperity gospel teaching.

It emphasizes the power of spoken words to create reality and shape one's circumstances. Here's an overview of positive confession and its role in the charismatic church:

Biblical Basis:

Positive confession is often based on scriptures such as Proverbs 18:21, which states, "Death and life are in the power of the tongue, and those who love it will eat its fruits."

Charismatic teachers interpret this and similar verses to mean that words have creative power and can influence one's destiny and circumstances.

Key Principles:

Positive confession teachings typically emphasize several fundamental principles:

Faith-filled Words:

Believers are encouraged to speak words of faith and affirmation in alignment with God's promises and purposes.

Declaration of Blessings:

Confessing blessings, health, prosperity, and success is believed to attract these realities into one's life.

Avoidance of Negative Speech:

Avoiding negative or pessimistic speech is essential to maintaining a positive confession lifestyle.

Prosperity Gospel Connection:

Positive confession is closely linked to the prosperity gospel, which teaches that God desires believers to be healthy, wealthy, and successful in every area of life.

According to this teaching, confessing positive words of faith and prosperity activates God's blessings and releases supernatural favor.

Criticism and Controversy:

Positive confession teachings have been criticized by some theologians, pastors, and Christian leaders for various reasons:

Reductionism:

Critics argue that positive confession reduces prayer and faith to a formulaic approach, minimizing the sovereignty of God and the complexities of human experience.

Materialism:

Some critics assert that positive confession teachings promote a materialistic and self-centered view of Christianity, focusing on personal gain rather than spiritual growth or service to others.

Lack of Scriptural Support:

Skeptics question the biblical basis of positive confession teachings, suggesting they misinterpret or cherry-pick verses to support their claims.

Impact on the Charismatic Church:

Positive confession teachings have significantly impacted the charismatic church, particularly within the prosperity gospel movement.

Many charismatic preachers and ministries incorporate positive confession principles into their teachings, encouraging believers to speak words of faith, success, and prosperity. These teachings have resonated with many believers seeking practical strategies for overcoming challenges and achieving their goals.

In summary, positive confession is a theological concept within the charismatic movement that emphasizes the power of spoken words to shape reality and attract blessings.

While it has been embraced by many believers as a means of activating faith and experiencing God's favor, it has also generated controversy and criticism within the broader Christian community for its perceived reductionism, materialism, and lack of biblical support.

Charismatic Authors and Literature

The charismatic church has produced numerous influential books that have impacted believers worldwide. These books cover many topics, including theology, spiritual growth, prayer, revival, and the supernatural.

Here are some of the most significant books that have emerged from the charismatic movement:

"The Holy Spirit and You" by Dennis Bennett:

Published in 1971, this book by Episcopal priest Dennis Bennett played a pivotal role in introducing the charismatic renewal movement to mainstream Christianity.

Bennett's personal testimony of experiencing the baptism in the Holy Spirit and speaking in tongues challenged traditional theological perspectives. It inspired countless believers to seek a deeper relationship with the Holy Spirit.

"Fresh Wind, Fresh Fire" by Jim Cymbala:

In this book, Pastor Jim Cymbala shares how God transformed his struggling Brooklyn church, the Brooklyn Tabernacle, into a thriving center of prayer, worship, and evangelism.

Published in 1997, "Fresh Wind, Fresh Fire" encourages believers to prioritize prayer and rely on the Holy Spirit's power for spiritual breakthroughs and revival in their lives and churches.

"Hosting the Presence" by Bill Johnson:

Bill Johnson, senior leader of Bethel Church in Redding, California, explores the concept of hosting God's presence in this influential book. Published in 2012, "Hosting the Presence" challenges believers to cultivate a lifestyle of intimacy with God, allowing His presence to transform their lives, relationships, and communities.

"Surprised by the Power of the Spirit" by Jack Deere:

Jack Deere, a former professor at Dallas Theological Seminary, shares his journey from skepticism to embracing the charismatic gifts of the Spirit in this groundbreaking book.

Published in 1993, "Surprised by the Power of the Spirit" provides a theological and experiential foundation for the charismatic gifts of prophecy, healing, and miracles, challenging traditional cessationist views.

"Prayer: Conversing with God" by Rosalind Rinker:

This classic book on prayer, first published in 1959, has taught believers how to develop a vibrant prayer life.

Rosalind Rinker's practical insights and heartfelt encouragement have inspired generations of Christians to deepen their intimacy with God through prayer.

"The Supernatural Power of a Transformed Mind" by Bill Johnson:

In this book, Bill Johnson explores the transformative power of renewing the mind according to God's Word.

Published in 2005, "The Supernatural Power of a Transformed Mind" challenges believers to align their thinking with Kingdom principles and to expect supernatural breakthroughs in every area of life.

These are just a few examples of the significant books that have emerged from the charismatic church, each contributing to the spiritual growth, theological understanding, and practical application of charismatic beliefs and practices among believers worldwide.

Good Morning, Holy Spirit:

Benny Hinn's book, "Good Morning, Holy Spirit," has been a cornerstone of the Charismatic Movement, offering insights into the person and work of the Holy Spirit.

Drawing from biblical scholarship and theological reflection, we evaluate Hinn's teachings on the Holy Spirit, highlighting areas of strength and potential concerns.

Additionally, it explores the book's influence on Christian spirituality and its implications for contemporary Christian practice.

Introduction:

"Good Morning, Holy Spirit" by Benny Hinn has been a widely influential book within the Charismatic Movement since its publication in 1990.

Let us analyze Hinn's book's theological content, practical implications, and overall impact on the Charismatic Movement and contemporary Christian spirituality.

By examining the book's teachings on the Holy Spirit in light of biblical scholarship and theological reflection, we aim to provide a balanced assessment of its strengths and potential concerns.

Theological Foundations:

"Good Morning, Holy Spirit" is grounded in a charismatic understanding of the Holy Spirit, emphasizing the personal relationship between believers and the third person of the Trinity.

Hinn presents the Holy Spirit as a divine person who desires to dwell within believers, empower them for ministry, and lead them into deeper intimacy with God. Drawing from biblical narratives and personal anecdotes, Hinn highlights the transformative power of the Holy Spirit in the lives of believers and the importance of cultivating sensitivity to His presence and guidance.

While Hinn's emphasis on the personal experience of the Holy Spirit resonates with many believers within the Charismatic Movement, some theologians have raised concerns about the book's lack of theological depth and nuance. Critics argue that Hinn's focus on subjective experiences and sensationalism may detract from a more robust understanding of pneumatology and the broader theological framework of the Christian faith.

Practical Implications:

"Good Morning, Holy Spirit" offers practical insights and spiritual exercises for believers seeking to deepen their relationship with the Holy Spirit.

Hinn encourages readers to cultivate a posture of openness and receptivity to the Spirit's leading, to pray for infilling the Spirit's power, and to practice spiritual disciplines such as prayer, worship, and fasting.

The book also includes testimonies of individuals who have experienced personal encounters with the Holy Spirit, illustrating the transformative impact of His presence in their lives.

While Hinn's practical guidance may be helpful for believers seeking a more profound experience of the Holy Spirit, some critics have raised concerns about the book's emphasis on emotionalism and experientialism at the expense of biblical discernment and theological reflection.

Critics argue that Hinn's focus on subjective experiences may lead to spiritual excesses and theological confusion, undermining the need for a balanced and discerning approach to the Christian life.

Impact on the Charismatic Movement:

"Good Morning, Holy Spirit" has significantly impacted the Charismatic Movement, shaping the beliefs and practices of countless believers worldwide.

The book's emphasis on the personal experience of the Holy Spirit, the importance of spiritual intimacy, and the power of prayer and worship has resonated with many within the Charismatic Movement, inspiring them to seek a more profound encounter with God's presence and power.

However, the book's influence has not been without controversy, as critics have raised concerns about Hinn's theology and ministry practices.

Some theologians and Christian leaders have questioned the theological soundness of Hinn's teachings on the Holy Spirit, citing potential inconsistencies with biblical doctrine and historical Christian orthodoxy.

Hinn's association with prosperity theology and his controversial ministry practices have also led to widespread criticism and scrutiny within the broader Christian community.

Conclusion:

In conclusion, "Good Morning, Holy Spirit" by Benny Hinn has been a seminal work within the Charismatic Movement, offering insights into the person and work of the Holy Spirit.

While the book has inspired many believers to seek a deeper relationship with the Spirit, it has also generated criticism and controversy due to its theological implications and the author's ministry practices.

As readers engage with Hinn's teachings on the Holy Spirit, it is essential to approach the book with discernment, drawing from biblical scholarship and theological reflection to evaluate its theological foundations and practical implications.

Ultimately, "Good Morning, Holy Spirit" invites believers to encounter the presence and power of the Holy Spirit in their lives and ministries, challenging them to live in obedience and submission to God's will.

The Charismatic Movement and Crusades

The term "crusades" in the context of the charismatic church typically refers to large-scale evangelistic events or revival meetings aimed at reaching the lost and ministering to believers.

These crusades often feature dynamic preaching, passionate worship, prayer, healing, and spiritual impartation opportunities.

Here's how the charismatic church engages with crusades:

Evangelistic Outreach:

Charismatic crusades are often organized with a primary focus on evangelism, seeking to reach those who have not heard the gospel or need spiritual renewal.

Charismatic preachers and evangelists use these events to proclaim the message of salvation, invite people to receive Jesus Christ as their Lord and Savior and lead them into a personal relationship with God.

Healing and Miracles:

Many charismatic crusades emphasize the supernatural power of God to heal the sick, deliver the oppressed, and perform miracles. Charismatic preachers often pray for the sick and lay hands on individuals, believing in the biblical promise of divine healing and restoration.

Testimonies of miraculous healings and encounters with God's power often play a central role in charismatic crusades, inspiring faith and drawing people to Christ.

Deliverance and Spiritual Warfare:

Charismatic crusades may also address issues of spiritual bondage, oppression, and demonic influence. Preachers may lead sessions on deliverance and spiritual warfare, teaching believers to overcome spiritual strongholds and walk in freedom and victory.

These sessions often involve prayer, repentance, and breaking generational curses and soul ties.

Empowerment and Equipping:

In addition to evangelism and ministry to the lost, charismatic crusades aim to empower and equip believers for ministry and spiritual growth. Charismatic preachers may teach on topics such as baptism in the Holy Spirit, the gifts of the Spirit, and the importance of living a life of faith and obedience to God's Word.

Believers are encouraged to step out in faith, use their spiritual gifts, and impact the Kingdom of God in their communities and spheres of influence.

Community and Unity:

Charismatic crusades often foster community and unity among believers from different churches and denominations.

These events unite Christians from diverse backgrounds and traditions, creating opportunities for fellowship, worship, and mutual encouragement.

Charismatic crusades catalyze relationships, strengthen partnerships, and mobilize the Body of Christ for collective action and ministry.

In summary, charismatic crusades are influential gatherings that combine evangelism, worship, healing, deliverance, and equipping to advance the Kingdom of God and impact lives for eternity.

The charismatic church seeks to fulfill the Great Commission proclaiming Jesus's gospel through these events.

The Charismatic Movement and the Word of Faith Movement

The charismatic church and the Word of Faith movement are closely intertwined, with the latter emerging as a significant theological and practical influence within charismatic Christianity.

Here's an overview of the relationship between the charismatic church and the Word of Faith movement:

Origins and Development:

The Word of Faith movement traces its origins to the teachings of early Pentecostal and charismatic leaders such as E.W. Kenyon, Kenneth Hagin, and Oral Roberts.

These leaders emphasized the power of faith, the authority of the believer, and the importance of positive confession in experiencing God's blessings and supernatural provision. Over time, their teachings evolved into a distinct theological framework known as the Word of Faith movement.

Key Tenets:

The Word of Faith movement emphasizes several vital tenets that have become central to charismatic theology and practice:

Faith:

Believers are taught that faith is a spiritual force or power that can be activated through belief and confession, enabling them to access God's blessings and supernatural provision.

Confession:

Positive confession is seen as a means of speaking God's promises into existence and aligning one's words with God's Word. Believers are encouraged to speak faith-filled affirmations and declarations to manifest desired outcomes.

Prosperity:

The Word of Faith movement teaches that God desires believers to experience abundance in every area of life, including health, finances, and relationships. Prosperity is a sign of God's favor and a natural outcome of faith-filled living.

Divine Healing:

Believers are taught that divine healing is part of the atonement provided by Christ and that they can receive healing through faith and confession. Many Word of Faith teachers emphasize the importance of believing and confessing God's promises for healing to receive physical restoration.

Influence on the Charismatic Church:

The Word of Faith movement has significantly influenced the charismatic church, shaping its theology, worship, and ministry practices.

Many charismatic churches and ministries incorporate Word of Faith teachings into their preaching and teaching, emphasizing the power of faith, confession, and positive thinking in experiencing God's blessings and supernatural interventions.

Word of Faith preachers and authors, such as Kenneth Copeland, Benny Hinn, and Creflo Dollar, are often featured speakers at charismatic conferences and events, further disseminating their teachings within the charismatic community.

Criticism and Controversy:

While the Word of Faith movement has garnered a large following within the charismatic church, it has also faced criticism and controversy.

Critics have raised concerns about the movement's emphasis on material prosperity, the potential for manipulating and exploiting vulnerable believers, and theological errors such as the prosperity gospel. Some have accused Word of Faith teachers of promoting a "name it and claim it" theology that can lead to unrealistic expectations and spiritual harm.

The Word of Faith movement has significantly influenced the charismatic church, shaping its theology and practice around the central tenets of faith, confession, prosperity, and divine healing.

While it has attracted a large following and brought hope and encouragement to many believers, it has also sparked debate and controversy within the broader Christian community.

The charismatic church and "the anointing."

The concept of "the anointing" is central to the charismatic church and plays a significant role in its theology and practice.

In charismatic Christianity, anointing is understood as the empowering presence and activity of the Holy Spirit in the life of a believer for ministry, service, and spiritual effectiveness.

Here's an overview of the charismatic church and the anointing:
Biblical Foundation:

The belief in the anointing is rooted in biblical teachings about the Holy Spirit's role in empowering believers for ministry. In the Old Testament, prophets, priests, and kings were anointed with oil to symbolize God's special empowerment for their respective roles (1 Samuel 16:13; Exodus 30:30).

Jesus, the ultimate Prophet, Priest, and King, was anointed by the Holy Spirit at his baptism and subsequently empowered for his ministry (Luke 4:18-19; Acts 10:38).

Empowerment for Ministry:

In the charismatic church, the anointing is understood as the Holy Spirit's supernatural enablement for believers to fulfill their calling and ministry.

This may include preaching, teaching, evangelism, prophetic ministry, healing, deliverance, and acts of service. The anointing empowers believers to operate in spiritual gifts and to minister effectively to others in the power of the Holy Spirit.

Manifestations of the Anointing:

The anointing is often accompanied by tangible manifestations such as a sense of power, presence, authority, supernatural signs, and wonders.

Charismatic believers may experience the anointing during prayer, worship, preaching, or ministry, sensing a heightened awareness of God's presence and activity.

Seeking and Cultivating the Anointing:

Charismatic Christians seek to cultivate and grow in the anointing through prayer, fasting, worship, and spiritual disciplines. They recognize the importance of intimacy with God and dependence on the Holy Spirit to manifest His power and presence in their lives and ministries.

Transfer of the Anointing:

In charismatic circles, there is a belief in transferring the anointing from one person to another through the laying on of hands or the ministry of anointed leaders. This concept is based on biblical examples such as Elijah and Elisha (2 Kings 2:9-15) and the apostles in the book of Acts (Acts 8:14-17; 19:6).

Discerning True and Counterfeit Anointings:

Charismatic believers are encouraged to discern genuine manifestations of the anointing from counterfeit or false manifestations.

They rely on biblical criteria, the Spirit's witness, and the Spirit's fruit to discern the authenticity of spiritual experiences and manifestations.

In summary, anointing is a foundational concept in the charismatic church, representing the empowering presence and activity of the Holy Spirit in the lives of believers for ministry, service, and spiritual effectiveness.

Charismatic Christians seek to cultivate, grow, and operate in the anointing as they fulfill their calling to advance God's Kingdom and minister to others in the power of the Holy Spirit.

The Charismatic Movement and Impartation

Impartation is a central aspect of the charismatic church, representing the transmission of spiritual gifts, anointing, and blessings from one believer to another through the power of the Holy Spirit.

This practice is rooted in biblical examples and empowers believers for ministry and service. Here's an overview of impartation in the charismatic church:

Biblical Foundation:

The concept of impartation has its roots in the Bible, where we see examples of spiritual leaders imparting blessings, anointing, and authority to others through the laying on of hands or through prophetic declarations.

For instance, Moses imparted his authority to Joshua before the Israelites entered the Promised Land (Numbers 27:18-23), and the apostles in the early church laid hands on believers to receive the Holy Spirit (Acts 8:17; 19:6).

Empowerment for Ministry:

In the charismatic church, impartation empowers believers to fulfill their calling and ministry.

Through the laying on of hands and prayer, believers may receive an impartation of spiritual gifts, such as prophecy, healing, discernment, or evangelism, enabling them to operate in greater effectiveness and anointing in their service to God and others.

Transmission of Anointing:

Impartation often involves anointing from one believer to another. Charismatic leaders who walk in a particular anointing or grace may lay hands on others, imparting that same anointing for ministry or service. This can include anointings for healing, deliverance, prophetic ministry, or leadership.

Activation of Gifts:

Impartation is also seen as a means of activating or awakening spiritual gifts that may be dormant or underdeveloped in believers.

Through the laying on of hands and prayer, believers may experience a release of spiritual power and enablement, leading to a greater manifestation of their gifts and abilities for the edification of the body of Christ.

Discipleship and Mentorship:

Impartation often occurs within the context of discipleship and mentorship relationships, where more seasoned believers impart wisdom, experience, and spiritual authority to those who are younger or less mature in their faith.

This can involve formal mentoring relationships and informal moments of prayer and ministry where believers receive impartation from spiritual leaders and mentors.

Cautions and Discernment:

While impartation is valued and practiced within the charismatic church, believers are encouraged to exercise discernment and caution. Not all impartation is genuine, and there is a need to discern the source and nature of spiritual experiences. Charismatic Christians rely on biblical principles, the witness of the Spirit, and the fruit of the Spirit to distinguish the authenticity of impartation experiences and the alignment of any imparted gifts with God's Word.

In summary, impartation is a foundational practice in the charismatic church, representing the transmission of spiritual gifts, anointing, and blessings from one believer to another through the power of the Holy Spirit.

Through impartation, believers are empowered, activated, and equipped for ministry and service, leading to greater effectiveness and fruitfulness in advancing God's Kingdom.

The Charismatic Movement and the receiving of mantels

In the charismatic church, the receiving of mantles is deeply rooted in biblical tradition and spiritual heritage. A mantle symbolizes authority, anointing, and spiritual inheritance passed from one individual to another. Here's an overview of how the charismatic church perceives and practices the receiving of mantles:

Biblical Foundation:

The concept of receiving mantles is rooted in various Bible stories and passages. In the Old Testament, we see examples of prophets like Elijah passing their mantle, or cloak, to their successors as a sign of spiritual authority and empowerment. For instance, Elijah passed his mantle to Elisha before being taken to heaven (2 Kings 2:9-15).

This act symbolized the transfer of prophetic authority and anointing from generation to generation.

Spiritual Inheritance:

Within the charismatic church, the receiving of mantles is often viewed as a means of receiving spiritual inheritance and carrying forward the legacy of those who have gone before.

Believers may receive mantles of anointing, authority, or specific callings as a spiritual inheritance from mentors, leaders, or spiritual forebears who have impacted their lives and ministries.

Activation of Gifts and Callings:

Receiving a mantle in the charismatic context is often associated with activating spiritual gifts and callings. When believers receive a mantle from a spiritual leader or mentor, they may experience greater empowerment and anointing for ministry, enabling them to operate in their gifts and callings with increased effectiveness and authority.

Recognition and Confirmation:

Receiving a mantle can serve as a recognition and confirmation of the recipient's calling and anointing by spiritual authorities or mentors.

It may affirm the recipient's readiness and preparedness to step into a new level of ministry or leadership, as well as their alignment with the purposes and plans of God for their lives.

Continuity of Ministry:

The receiving of mantles also emphasizes the continuity of ministry and the passing of the torch from one generation to the next.

As believers receive mantles from spiritual leaders and mentors, they become part of a spiritual lineage and heritage, carrying forward the work of God's Kingdom and advancing His purposes on earth.

Cautions and Discernment:

While the receiving of mantles is valued and practiced within the charismatic church, believers are encouraged to exercise discernment and caution.

Not all claims of mantle-receiving may be genuine, and there is a need to discern the source and nature of such experiences. Charismatic Christians rely on biblical principles, the witness of the Spirit, and the fruit of the Spirit to distinguish the authenticity and alignment of any received mantles with God's Word and purposes.

In summary, receiving mantles in the charismatic church is a significant practice reflecting the biblical tradition of passing spiritual inheritance and authority from one generation to the next.

It emphasizes the activation of gifts and callings, recognition and confirmation of ministry, and the continuity of God's work through His people across generations.

The Charismatic Movement and alternative Bible translations and editions

In the charismatic church, there is often a wide acceptance and usage of alternative Bible translations and editions alongside traditional versions such as the King James Version (KJV).

Here's an overview of how the charismatic church views and utilizes alternative Bible translations and editions:

Accessibility and Clarity:

One reason for the popularity of alternative Bible translations and editions in the charismatic church is their accessibility and clarity of language.

While the KJV has been cherished for its literary beauty and historical significance, its archaic language can be challenging for modern readers to understand. Alternative translations, such as the New International Version (NIV), English Standard Version (ESV), or New Living Translation (NLT), offer contemporary language that is easier to comprehend, making the Bible more accessible to a broader audience.

Contextual Accuracy:

Charismatic Christians value Bible translations and editions that prioritize contextual accuracy and readability. They recognize the importance of accurately conveying the original meaning and intent of the biblical text while also making it relevant and understandable to contemporary readers. Alternative translations often use a combination of modern language and scholarly research to achieve this balance, ensuring that the message of the Bible is communicated effectively without sacrificing accuracy.

Emphasis on Application and Relevance:

In the charismatic church, there is a strong emphasis on the practical application of Scripture and its relevance to everyday life.

Alternative translations and editions often provide helpful study notes, commentaries, and application-focused features that aid believers in understanding and applying God's Word to their lives. These resources can enhance personal devotional study, small group discussions, and teaching ministries within the charismatic community.

Diverse Theological Perspectives:

Another factor influencing alternative Bible translations and editions in the charismatic church is the diversity of theological perspectives and doctrinal emphases within the movement.

While certain translations may align more closely with specific theological traditions or doctrinal interpretations, charismatic Christians appreciate the variety of translations available, each offering unique insights and perspectives on the biblical text.

Spiritual Growth and Discipleship:

Charismatic believers value Bible translations and editions that facilitate spiritual growth, discipleship, and deeper intimacy with God. Whether through study Bibles, devotional editions, or audio versions, alternative translations and editions provide tools and resources that support believers in their journey of faith, helping them to grow in knowledge, maturity, and relationship with God.

Personal Preference and Conviction:

Ultimately, the choice of Bible translation and edition is often a matter of personal preference and conviction for charismatic Christians. While some may prefer the literary beauty and tradition of the KJV, others may gravitate towards more modern translations for their clarity and accessibility.

The charismatic church values the diversity of translations and editions available, recognizing that each has strengths and benefits for spiritual growth and understanding God's Word.

The Use of the Passion Translation in the Charismatic Movement

Introduction:

The Passion Translation (TPT) has gained popularity within the Charismatic Movement as a contemporary, dynamic translation of the Bible that seeks to capture the passion and emotion of the original texts. Created by Dr. Brian Simmons, TPT has sparked enthusiasm and controversy among believers, particularly within charismatic circles.

The Passion Translation is extensively used within the Charismatic Movement. Let us examine its origins, reception, and impact on how Scripture is understood and interpreted within charismatic theology and spirituality.

Origins of the Passion Translation:

The Passion Translation emerged from the vision of Dr. Brian Simmons to create a translation of the Bible that would convey the original meaning and emotion of the biblical texts freshly and dynamically.

Drawing from his background as a linguist, missionary, and pastor, Simmons embarked on the ambitious task of translating the Bible with a focus on capturing the heart and passion of God's Word.

Simmons began by translating the New Testament, drawing from the Greek text, and consulting various translations and commentaries to ensure accuracy and fidelity to the original languages.

The resulting translation, known as The Passion Translation, was first published in 2009 and has since been expanded to include the Psalms, Proverbs, and other books of the Old Testament.

Reception Within the Charismatic Movement:

The Passion Translation has been embraced by many within the Charismatic Movement for its poetic language, vibrant imagery, and emphasis on the emotional depth of Scripture. Charismatic believers appreciate the passion and enthusiasm with which TPT presents the

Word of God, finding it a powerful tool for personal devotion, worship, and prayer.

TPT's focus on the heart and emotion of the biblical texts resonates with the experiential and emotive spirituality of the Charismatic Movement, inviting believers into a more profound encounter with God's presence and truth.

Many charismatic leaders and ministries have endorsed TPT, incorporating it into their teaching, preaching, and worship services as a means of conveying the passion and power of Scripture.

Critiques and Concerns:

Despite its popularity, the Passion Translation has also been met with criticism and concern within the Charismatic Movement and the broader Christian community. Some scholars and theologians have raised questions about the accuracy and reliability of TPT, noting its departure from traditional translation principles and its tendency to prioritize poetic expression over linguistic precision.

Critics argue that TPT's interpretive choices and paraphrasing can sometimes obscure the original meaning of the biblical texts, leading to theological distortions or misunderstandings.

Additionally, concerns have been raised about Dr. Brian Simmons' claims regarding his qualifications and experiences as a translator, as well as his assertion of receiving direct divine revelations during the translation process.

Impact on Charismatic Theology and Spirituality:

The use of the Passion Translation has significantly impacted charismatic theology and spirituality, shaping the way believers engage with Scripture and understand God's Word.

TPT's emphasis on passion, intimacy, and encounter with God resonates with the experiential and relational spirituality of the Charismatic Movement, deepening believers' appreciation for the emotional depth and personal relevance of Scripture.

TPT has also influenced charismatic interpretations of biblical prophecy, spiritual warfare, and the supernatural, as believers seek to apply its passionate and poetic language to understand God's plan for the end times and their role in advancing God's kingdom on earth.

The translation's vibrant imagery and evocative language have inspired believers to pursue a deeper relationship with God and to live out their faith with passion and zeal.

Conclusion:

The Passion Translation has become a significant resource within the Charismatic Movement, offering believers a fresh and dynamic perspective on the Word of God. While it has been praised for its poetic language and emotive expression, TPT has also generated controversy and debate over its accuracy and reliability as a translation of Scripture.

As believers continue to engage with the Passion Translation, it is crucial to approach it with discernment and humility, testing its interpretations against the broader context of biblical scholarship and theological tradition. While TPT can enrich our understanding and experience of Scripture, it should be used alongside other translations and resources to ensure a comprehensive and faithful interpretation of God's Word within the context of the Charismatic Movement.

The Charismatic Movement and "Do not touch God's anointed."

In the charismatic church, "do not touch God's anointed" is often used to emphasize the importance of showing respect and honor to spiritual leaders, especially those believed to be anointed or appointed by God for ministry. Here's an overview of how the charismatic church interprets and applies this principle:

Biblical Basis:

The phrase "do not touch God's anointed" is derived from passages in the Bible, particularly from the Old Testament. Psalm 105:15 says, "Touch not my anointed ones; do my prophets no harm."

Similarly, 1 Chronicles 16:22 warns, "Do not touch my anointed ones; do my prophets no harm."

Protection of Leaders:

In the charismatic church, the principle of "do not touch God's anointed" is often interpreted as a warning against speaking or acting in a harmful or critical manner towards spiritual leaders. Believers are encouraged to respect the authority and anointing God has placed on these leaders and to refrain from gossip, slander, or divisive behavior that could undermine their ministry or reputation.

Spiritual Authority:

Charismatic Christians believe in the concept of spiritual authority, where God appoints and anoints specific individuals to lead and minister to His people. These leaders, whether pastors, prophets, evangelists, or apostles, are seen as representatives of God and are entrusted with shepherding and guiding His flock. "Do not touch God's anointed" is often used to remind believers of the sacredness of this calling and the need to honor and submit to spiritual authority.

Accountability and Discernment:

While the principle of "do not touch God's anointed" emphasizes respect for spiritual leaders, it does not absolve them from accountability or scrutiny.

Charismatic Christians recognize the importance of holding leaders accountable to biblical standards of integrity, humility, and character. However, this accountability should be exercised with wisdom, grace, and discernment, avoiding slanderous accusations or judgmental attitudes that could cause harm or division within the body of Christ.

Teaching on Submission:

The principle of "do not touch God's anointed" is often accompanied by teachings on the importance of submission and obedience to spiritual authority.

Believers are encouraged to honor and pray for their leaders, trusting that God has placed them in their positions for His purposes and glory. At the same time, leaders are exhorted to shepherd God's flock with humility, love, and accountability, recognizing their need for God's grace and guidance.

Balanced Perspective:

While the charismatic church upholds the principle of "do not touch God's anointed" as a reminder of the sacredness of spiritual leadership, it also encourages a balanced perspective that acknowledges the fallibility of human leaders and the ultimate authority of God's Word.

Believers are called to exercise discernment, test everything against Scripture, and follow Christ above any human leader or authority.

In summary, "do not touch God's anointed" is a principle in the charismatic church that emphasizes respect for spiritual leaders and the need for accountability, discernment, and submission within the body of Christ.

It serves as a reminder of the sacred trust placed on those called to leadership roles and the responsibility of leaders and followers to honor God and His purposes in all things.

The Charismatic Movement and Personal Revelation

In the charismatic church, personal revelation refers to the belief that individual believers can receive direct guidance, insight, or understanding from God through the Holy Spirit apart from, or in addition to, the Scriptures. Here's an overview of how the charismatic church views and practices personal revelation:

Biblical Basis:

Charismatic Christians believe in the ongoing work of the Holy Spirit in the lives of believers, as described in the New Testament. Scriptures such as John 16:13, which promises that the Holy Spirit will guide believers into all truth, and 1 Corinthians 2:10-13, which speaks of the Spirit revealing spiritual truths to believers, are often cited as biblical support for personal revelation.

Indwelling Presence of the Holy Spirit:

Charismatic theology emphasizes the indwelling presence of the Holy Spirit in the lives of believers.

This belief leads to the conviction that God can speak directly to individuals through the promptings, impressions, or insights of the Holy Spirit.

Personal revelation is seen as a natural outworking of the believer's relationship with God and their sensitivity to the leading of the Spirit.

Subjective Nature:

Personal revelation is inherently subjective, as it involves the individual's perception of what they believe God is saying to them. Charismatic

Christians acknowledge the need for discernment and testing of personal revelation against biblical truth, the witness of the Spirit, and the counsel of mature believers.

While personal revelation can provide valuable guidance and encouragement, it is not considered authoritative or equivalent to Scripture.

Forms of Personal Revelation:

Personal revelation can take various forms within the charismatic church, including:

Prophetic Words:

Believers may receive prophetic words or messages from God through the gift of prophecy. These messages can offer encouragement, direction, correction, or insight into specific situations or circumstances.

Dreams and Visions:

Charismatic Christians believe that God can speak to individuals through dreams and visions, revealing His will or purposes for their lives.

Inner Witness:

Personal revelation can also come through inner peace, conviction, or assurance that a particular course of action is aligned with God's will.

Confirmation:

Sometimes, personal revelation serves as confirmation of truths or guidance already revealed in Scripture or through other means.

Community Accountability:

While personal revelation is valued within the charismatic church, believers are encouraged to exercise accountability within the community of faith.

This includes submitting personal revelations to the oversight of spiritual leaders, testing them against Scripture, and seeking confirmation or discernment from other mature believers.

Caution and Discernment:

Charismatic Christians recognize the need for caution and discernment in interpreting personal revelation. They know the potential for subjective biases, human error, or even deception in receiving and interpreting personal revelation. Therefore, believers are encouraged to weigh personal revelation carefully and humbly, remaining open to correction and guidance from God and His Word.

In summary, personal revelation is a significant aspect of the charismatic church's understanding of the believer's relationship with God and the work of the Holy Spirit in their lives. While valued as a means of receiving guidance and encouragement from God, personal revelation is subject to testing, discernment, and accountability within the context of the broader Christian community and the authority of Scripture.

Charismatic Buzzwords

Anointed Worship:

Refers to worship experiences where the Holy Spirit's presence is tangibly felt, leading to deep spiritual encounters, emotional responses, and personal transformation. Scriptural reference: "God is spirit, and his worshipers must worship in the Spirit and in truth." (John 4:24)

Anointing:

The anointing refers to the empowering presence of the Holy Spirit upon an individual for ministry or service. It is believed to enable believers to perform God's work effectively. Scriptural reference: "But you have an anointing from the Holy One, and all of you know the truth." (1 John 2:20)

Baptism in the Holy Spirit:

This is an experience subsequent to salvation where believers receive a fuller measure of the Holy Spirit's power and presence. It's often associated with speaking in tongues. Scriptural reference: "I baptize you with water for repentance. But after me comes one who is more powerful than I, whose sandals I am not worthy to carry. He will baptize you with the Holy Spirit and fire." (Matthew 3:11)

Breakthrough Prayer:

Prayer that is fervent, persistent, and faith-filled, often directed towards overcoming obstacles, strongholds, or barriers hindering spiritual growth or advancement. Scriptural reference: "And pray in the Spirit on all occasions with all kinds of prayers and requests. With this in mind, be alert and always keep on praying for all the Lord's people." (Ephesians 6:18)

Divine Appointment:

Refers to the belief that certain meetings, encounters, or events are arranged by God for specific purposes or divine interventions. Scriptural reference: "For we are God's handiwork, created in Christ

Jesus to do good works, which God prepared in advance for us to do."
(Ephesians 2:10)

Divine Encounter:

This refers to personal experiences of encountering God's presence, often characterized by a sense of awe, reverence, and intimacy, and leading to deeper spiritual insight and transformation. Scriptural reference: "In the year that King Uzziah died, I saw the Lord, high and exalted, seated on a throne; and the train of his robe filled the temple." (Isaiah 6:1)

Divine Favor:

Refers to God's gracious and undeserved kindness, blessings, or preferential treatment toward His people, often resulting in opportunities, provision, and success beyond human merit. Scriptural reference: "For you bless the righteous, O Lord; you cover him with favor as with a shield." (Psalm 5:12)

Divine Manifestation:

Refers to the tangible display or revelation of God's presence, power, or glory in a particular place, event, or individual's life, often leading to awe, reverence, and worship. Scriptural reference: "And the glory of the Lord shall be revealed, and all flesh shall see it together, for the mouth of the Lord has spoken." (Isaiah 40:5)

Divine Revelation:

Describes the unveiling or disclosure of spiritual truths, mysteries, or insights by God, often communicated through Scripture, dreams, visions, or prophetic utterances. Scriptural reference: "The secret things belong to the Lord our God, but the things revealed belong to us and to our children forever, that we may follow all the words of this law." (Deuteronomy 29:29)

Fire Tunnel:

A symbolic or literal passage formed by individuals laying hands on others in prayer, often believed to release an impartation of the Holy Spirit's power or anointing. Scriptural reference: "When the day of

Pentecost came, they were all together in one place. Suddenly a sound like the blowing of a violent wind came from heaven and filled the whole house where they were sitting." (Acts 2:1-2)

Fruit of the Spirit:

Describes the character traits and virtues produced in the lives of believers by the indwelling of the Holy Spirit, such as love, joy, peace, patience, kindness, goodness, faithfulness, gentleness, and self-control. Scriptural reference: "But the fruit of the Spirit is love, joy, peace, forbearance, kindness, goodness, faithfulness, gentleness and self-control. Against such things there is no law." (Galatians 5:22-23)

Glory Cloud:

An atmospheric phenomenon or spiritual experience where a visible manifestation of God's presence, often described as a cloud or mist, is perceived during worship or prayer gatherings. Scriptural reference: "Then the cloud covered the tent of meeting, and the glory of the Lord filled the tabernacle." (Exodus 40:34)

Glory Encounter:

An experience of encountering the manifest presence of God, often accompanied by a sense of awe, reverence, and transformation. Scriptural reference: "But we all, with unveiled face, beholding as in a mirror the glory of the Lord, are being transformed into the same image from glory to glory, just as by the Spirit of the Lord." (2 Corinthians 3:18)

Healing Ministry:

This refers to the belief in God's power to heal physical, emotional, and spiritual ailments through prayer, laying on of hands, and anointing with oil. Scriptural reference: "And these signs will accompany those who believe: In my name they will drive out demons; they will speak in new tongues; they will pick up snakes with their hands; and when they drink deadly poison, it will not hurt them at all; they will place their hands on sick people, and they will get well." (Mark 16:17-18)

Heavenly Downloads:

This term is often used to describe sudden insights, revelations, or inspirations believed to be directly imparted by the Holy Spirit, providing divine wisdom or understanding. Scriptural reference: "Call to me and I will answer you and tell you great and unsearchable things you do not know." (Jeremiah 33:3)

Heavenly Realms:

This term describes the spiritual dimension where God's presence, authority, and kingdom rule are experienced, often emphasized in teachings about spiritual warfare and prophetic encounters. Scriptural reference: "Our struggle is not against flesh and blood, but against the rulers, against the authorities, against the powers of this dark world and against the spiritual forces of evil in the heavenly realms." (Ephesians 6:12)

Impartation:

The belief in the transfer or imparting of spiritual gifts, anointing, or blessings from one person to another through laying on of hands, prayer, or prophetic action. Scriptural reference: "For this reason I remind you to fan into flame the gift of God, which is in you through the laying on of my hands." (2 Timothy 1:6)

Kingdom Advancement:

The collective effort and focus of believers towards spreading the message of God's kingdom, bringing about transformation in society, and fulfilling the Great Commission. Scriptural reference: "But seek first his kingdom and his righteousness, and all these things will be given to you as well." (Matthew 6:33)

Kingdom Impact:

Describes the transformative influence and effect that believers, empowered by the Holy Spirit, have on their surroundings, communities, and spheres of influence, advancing God's kingdom agenda. Scriptural reference: "You are the salt of the earth... You are the light of the world." (Matthew 5:13-14)

Open Heaven:

The belief in an atmosphere or spiritual condition where the barrier between heaven and earth is perceived as thin or nonexistent, facilitating a greater flow of God's presence, revelation, and supernatural activity. Scriptural reference: "Heaven opened and the Holy Spirit descended on him in bodily form like a dove." (Luke 3:21-22)

Overflowing Abundance:

Refers to experiencing an abundance or overflow of God's blessings, provision, or favor in one's life, often beyond what is expected or imagined. Scriptural reference: "Now to him who is able to do immeasurably more than all we ask or imagine, according to his power that is at work within us." (Ephesians 3:20)

Power Encounter:

Refers to confrontations or situations where God's power is visibly demonstrated, often through miracles, healings, or deliverance from demonic oppression, leading to spiritual breakthroughs and transformations. Scriptural reference: "For our gospel came to you not simply with words but also with power, with the Holy Spirit and deep conviction." (1 Thessalonians 1:5)

Power of Agreement:

This concept highlights the spiritual principle of unity in prayer and belief among believers, emphasizing the effectiveness of collective faith and agreement in aligning with God's will. Scriptural reference: "Again, truly I tell you that if two of you on earth agree about anything they ask for, it will be done for them by my Father in heaven." (Matthew 18:19)

Presence-Centered Worship:

Emphasizes the importance of focusing on God's presence during worship gatherings, seeking intimacy, encounter, and transformation through worship rather than mere performance or ritual. Scriptural reference: "In your presence there is fullness of joy; at your right hand are pleasures forevermore." (Psalm 16:11)

Prophetic Activation:

Involves exercises or activities designed to cultivate, develop, or sharpen prophetic gifts and abilities within believers, such as practicing hearing God's voice, interpreting dreams, or delivering prophetic words. Scriptural reference: "Do not quench the Spirit. Do not treat prophecies with contempt but test them all; hold on to what is good." (1 Thessalonians 5:19-21)

Prophetic Decree:

Refers to authoritative declarations made under the inspiration of the Holy Spirit, often spoken with confidence and faith to proclaim God's purposes, blessings, or judgments over individuals, situations, or regions. Scriptural reference: "You shall also decree a thing, and it shall be established unto you: and the light shall shine upon your ways." (Job 22:28)

Prophetic Insight:

Involves receiving and interpreting revelations, visions, or messages from God about future events, spiritual truths, or personal guidance, often shared with others for edification or warning. Scriptural reference: "Surely the Lord God does nothing, Unless He reveals His secret to His servants the prophets." (Amos 3:7)

Prophetic Intercession:

This involves praying with insights and direction from the Holy Spirit, often concerning specific situations, individuals, or events. Scriptural reference: "The prayer of a righteous person is powerful and effective." (James 5:16)

Prophetic Release:

Involves the act of releasing or imparting prophetic words, blessings, or declarations over individuals, groups, or situations, often believed to carry God's power and authority for transformation.

Scriptural reference: "Death and life are in the power of the tongue, And those who love it will eat its fruit." (Proverbs 18:21)

Prophetic Word:

This refers to a message or revelation believed to be directly from God, often spoken by individuals under the influence of the Holy Spirit. Scriptural reference: "But the one who prophesies speaks to people for their strengthening, encouraging and comfort." (1 Corinthians 14:3)

Prophetic Worship:

A form of worship characterized by spontaneity, freedom, and openness to the leading of the Holy Spirit, often involving prophetic utterances, songs, and expressions. Scriptural reference: "But the hour is coming, and is now here, when the true worshipers will worship the Father in spirit and truth, for the Father is seeking such people to worship him." (John 4:23)

Revival:

A period of renewed spiritual interest and activity within the church, often characterized by intense worship, repentance, and a hunger for God's presence. Scriptural reference: "Will you not revive us again, that your people may rejoice in you?" (Psalm 85:6)

Speaking in Tongues:

This refers to the practice of speaking in a language unknown to the speaker, often interpreted as a sign of being filled with the Holy Spirit. Scriptural reference: "They were all filled with the Holy Spirit and began to speak in other tongues as the Spirit enabled them." (Acts 2:4)

Spiritual Acceleration:

Refers to a rapid or intensified growth, advancement, or manifestation of spiritual maturity and fruitfulness in one's life, often attributed to the work of the Holy Spirit. Scriptural reference: "But grow in the grace and knowledge of our Lord and Savior Jesus Christ." (2 Peter 3:18)

Spiritual Activation:

The process or experience of stirring up, activating, or unleashing spiritual gifts, potentials, or abilities within oneself or others through prayer, impartation, or prophetic declaration. Scriptural reference: "For this reason I remind you to fan into flame the gift of God, which is in you through the laying on of my hands." (2 Timothy 1:6)

Spiritual Alignment:

This concept emphasizes the importance of being in harmony with God's will, purposes, and character, and aligning one's thoughts, actions, and desires accordingly through prayer, meditation, and obedience. Scriptural reference: "But seek first the kingdom of God and his righteousness, and all these things will be added to you." (Matthew 6:33)

Spiritual Atmosphere:

Refers to the prevailing spiritual climate or environment in a particular place, gathering, or situation, influenced by the presence, activity, and manifestation of the Holy Spirit and characterized by peace, joy, and reverence. Scriptural reference: "For where two or three gather in my name, there am I with them." (Matthew 18:20)

Spiritual Awakening:

Similar to revival, it signifies a widespread renewal of spiritual fervor and commitment, both within the church and in society at large. Scriptural reference: "Awake, O sleeper, and arise from the dead, and Christ will shine on you." (Ephesians 5:14)

Spiritual Breakthrough:

This refers to overcoming spiritual barriers or obstacles through prayer, fasting, and faith, leading to personal or collective growth and advancement in one's relationship with God. Scriptural reference: "For though we live in the world, we do not wage war as the world does. The weapons we fight with are not the weapons of the world. On the contrary, they have divine power to demolish strongholds." (2 Corinthians 10:3-4)

Spiritual Discernment:

The ability to distinguish between spiritual truths and deceptions, and to recognize the movement of the Holy Spirit in various situations. Scriptural reference: "But solid food is for the mature, for those who have their powers of discernment trained by constant practice to distinguish good from evil." (Hebrews 5:14)

Spiritual Empowerment:

This term denotes the endowment or infusion of spiritual strength, authority, or gifting from the Holy Spirit, enabling believers to fulfill their God-given purposes and ministry assignments. Scriptural reference: "But you will receive power when the Holy Spirit comes on you; and you will be my witnesses in Jerusalem, and in all Judea and Samaria, and to the ends of the earth." (Acts 1:8)

Spiritual Fulfillment:

This term describes the deep satisfaction, contentment, and purpose found in one's relationship with God and alignment with His will, often contrasted with worldly pursuits or temporary pleasures. Scriptural reference: "You make known to me the path of life; you will fill me with joy in your presence, with eternal pleasures at your right hand." (Psalm 16:11)

Spiritual Gifts:

These are special abilities given by the Holy Spirit to believers for the edification of the church and the advancement of God's kingdom. Examples include prophecy, healing, and speaking in tongues. Scriptural reference: "Now to each one the manifestation of the Spirit is given for the common good." (1 Corinthians 12:7)

Spiritual Inheritance:

Describes the blessings, promises, and spiritual benefits received by believers as children of God, including salvation, eternal life, and an abundant life in Christ. Scriptural reference: "Blessed be the God and Father of our Lord Jesus Christ, who has blessed us with every spiritual blessing in the heavenly places in Christ." (Ephesians 1:3)

Spiritual Intimacy:

Describes the depth of personal relationship and closeness with God, often pursued through prayer, worship, and meditation on Scripture, resulting in a profound sense of communion and connection with the Divine. Scriptural reference: "Draw near to God, and he will draw near to you." (James 4:8)

Spiritual Mentorship:

This concept involves the guidance, discipleship, and nurturing of spiritual growth provided by more experienced or mature believers to younger or less mature believers, fostering accountability, growth, and maturity. Scriptural reference: "And the things you have heard me say in the presence of many witnesses entrust to reliable people who will also be qualified to teach others." (2 Timothy 2:2)

Spiritual Momentum:

Describes the sense of spiritual progress, advancement, or acceleration experienced by believers as they grow in faith, obedience, and intimacy with God, leading to increased effectiveness and impact in their lives and ministries. Scriptural reference: "But those who hope in the Lord will renew their strength. They will soar on wings like eagles; they will run and not grow weary, they will walk and not be faint." (Isaiah 40:31)

Spiritual Overflow:

Refers to an abundance or surplus of spiritual blessings, joy, and vitality experienced by believers as a result of their intimate relationship with God and being filled with the Holy Spirit. Scriptural reference: "You prepare a table before me in the presence of my enemies; you anoint my head with oil; my cup overflows." (Psalm 23:5)

Spiritual Refreshing:

This term refers to a renewal or revitalization of one's spiritual life, often experienced through times of intimate worship, prayer, and seeking God's presence. Scriptural reference: "Repent, then, and turn to

God, so that your sins may be wiped out, that times of refreshing may come from the Lord." (Acts 3:19)

Spiritual Renewal:

Describes a revitalization or restoration of one's spiritual vitality, passion, or commitment, often experienced through times of repentance, revival, and seeking God's presence. Scriptural reference: "Create in me a clean heart, O God, and renew a steadfast spirit within me." (Psalm 51:10)

Spiritual Resilience:

Describes the ability to endure and persevere through trials, challenges, or spiritual attacks, relying on God's strength, grace, and promises to overcome adversity and grow in faith. Scriptural reference: "Consider it pure joy, my brothers and sisters, whenever you face trials of many kinds, because you know that the testing of your faith produces perseverance." (James 1:2-3)

Spiritual Sensitivity:

Refers to the heightened awareness, discernment, and responsiveness to the leading and prompting of the Holy Spirit in one's life, enabling believers to recognize and cooperate with God's work. Scriptural reference: "But when he, the Spirit of truth, comes, he will guide you into all the truth." (John 16:13)

Spiritual Stirring:

This term denotes a deep inner prompting, urging, or awakening of spiritual hunger, passion, or zeal within an individual or a group, often leading to a desire for deeper intimacy with God and greater commitment to His purposes. Scriptural reference: "For this reason, I remind you to fan into flame the gift of God, which is in you through the laying on of my hands." (2 Timothy 1:6)

Spiritual Transference:

The belief in the transfer or impartation of spiritual blessings, anointing, or authority from one person to another through laying on of hands, prophetic declaration, or spiritual mentoring. Scriptural reference: "The things you have heard me say in the presence of many witnesses entrust to reliable people who will also be qualified to teach others." (2 Timothy 2:2)

Spiritual Warfare:

This is the belief in engaging in spiritual battles against demonic forces through prayer, fasting, and other spiritual disciplines. Scriptural reference: "For our struggle is not against flesh and blood, but against the rulers, against the authorities, against the powers of this dark world and against the spiritual forces of evil in the heavenly realms." (Ephesians 6:12)

Spiritual Warfare Strategies:

Refers to the various tactics, prayers, and spiritual disciplines employed by believers to combat and overcome spiritual opposition, demonic influence, and negative forces. Scriptural reference: "For though we live in the world, we do not wage war as the world does. The weapons we fight with are not the weapons of the world." (2 Corinthians 10:3-4)

Supernatural Intervention:

Describes divine intervention or involvement in human affairs, often manifested through miracles, signs, or wonders, and believed to be a demonstration of God's power and sovereignty. Scriptural reference: "Jesus looked at them and said, 'With man this is impossible, but with God all things are possible.'" (Matthew 19:26)

Supernatural Provision:

Refers to the belief in God's ability to provide for all the needs of His people beyond natural means, often cited in contexts of financial blessings, miraculous interventions, and divine provision. Scriptural reference: "And my God will meet all your needs according to the riches of his glory in Christ Jesus." (Philippians 4:19)

Don't miss out!

Visit the website below and you can sign up to receive emails whenever Carl Davis publishes a new book. There's no charge and no obligation.

https://books2read.com/r/B-A-ZAXZ-VDJBD

BOOKS 2 READ

Connecting independent readers to independent writers.

Also by Carl Davis

Ek, is Dawid Soeker

A Brief History Of Christianity In Africa

Icing the Eskimo - The Art of Aggressive Sales

Nuclear Faith

Toxic Pulpit

Van Paradegrond tot Pastorie

Group Dynamics and Motivation

Pastoral counselling models for perinatal and postpartum episodes

Basic New Testament Survey

So......You want to be a Waiter

Eternal Logos: The Evolution of Scriptural Interpretation: From Ancient Methodology to Postmodern Perspectives

Ewige Woord Die Evolusie van Skrifuitleg: Van Antieke Metodiek tot Postmoderne Perspektiewe

Teaching Ministry

The Funny Side Of Reasoning - Fallacies, principles and typologies in the modern business world.

Passion Unleashed: Igniting The Future With Purpose.

Esther: Triumph of Courage and Divine Providence

Chronicles of Grace: An Epic Journey through 1 & 2 Samuel

Fire and Faith: Navigating the Charismatic Movement in the Modern World

About the Author

Carl Davis holds a Doctorate in Missiology based upon research of Organizational Growth in the Post Modern Society.I started my work life serving in the South African Defence Force – first at the Recruiting Division, then moving to a Medical Command where I served as a Generalist Personnel Officer. For the last two years of my service, I was tasked with the Personnel management of the Integration process, inclusive of entrance and exit strategies.After honorable discharge after more than 10 years in the South African Defence Force, I took up the post of Managing Director of a Non-Government Organization, established to uplift impoverished communities in and around Potchefstroom, while also appointed as a part-time lecturer of undergraduates (specifically on leadership).Three years later I was appointed as Rector, managing an Educational Institute with 4000 students spread over 36 African countries. While in this position I had the opportunity to lecture extensively abroad and published various articles on leadership; with specific emphasis on motivation and group dynamics. I am a strong believer in utilizing a blended and integrated approach in all of the training (including the new material which I developed) I developed which included – Leadership (within a Faith based community), andragogy, and Cultural Diversity management.I am also a graduate of the University of Stellenbosch's Facilitative Leadership Programme (BUVTON), consulting and facilitating with organizations that are "stuck" (- Alice Mann 1998-) specifically in the process of change management.